High-Functioning Autism and Difficult Moments

High-Functioning Autism and Difficult Moments

Practical Solutions for Reducing Meltdowns

Brenda Smith Myles, Ph.D., and Ruth Aspy, Ph.D.

PUBLISHING

11209 Strang Line Rd.
Lenexa, Kansas 66215
www.aapcpublishing.net

11209 Strang Line Rd.
Lenexa, Kansas 66215
www.aapcpublishing.net

Publisher's Cataloging-in-Publication

Names:	Myles, Brenda Smith, author. | Aspy, Ruth, author.
Title:	High-functioning autism and difficult moments : practical solutions for reducing meltdowns / Brenda Smith Myles, Ph.D. and Ruth Aspy, Ph.D.
Description:	Lenexa, Kansas : AAPC Publishing, [2016] | Includes bibliographical references.
Identifiers:	ISBN: 978-1-942197-24-9 | LCCN: 2016937489
Subjects:	LCSH: Autism spectrum disorders in children--Treatment. | Child psychology. | Behavior disorders in children--Treatment. | Autism spectrum disorders--Patients--Rehabilitation. | Asperger's syndrome in children--Treatment. | Sensory integration dysfunction in children--Treatment. | Stress management for children. | Behavioral assessment. | Children--Behavior modification.

Classification: LCC: RJ506.A9 M976 2016 \| DDC: 618.92/85882--dc23

This book is designed in Myriad Pro.

Printed in the United States of America.

Contents

Characteristics of Individuals With High-Functioning Autism Spectrum Disorder – Current Neurological Research Findings

By now, almost everyone who has lived with, worked with, befriended, supported a person on the spectrum, or is on the spectrum, realizes that the behaviors that we consider to be "autistic" – such as flapping, repeating words or sentences, flinching around loud noises, and focusing on a topic for a long time – are strategies used to cope with a world that can be unfriendly and overwhelming. And often, these strategies are the only ones the person with high-functioning autism spectrum disorder (HF-ASD) has available in a given situation. In addition, thanks to current research in autism, which is dominated by neurological studies, we have come to understand that "autistic behaviors" are brain-based.

This brief chapter will review some of the neurological research on HF-ASD and its connection – directly and indirectly – to meltdowns. This is in no way meant to be a comprehensive review of the literature on the autistic neurology. The aim of this chapter is to allow readers to see the relationships between neurology and behaviors in

HF-ASD with a focus on practical applications, specifically, to prevent those who support individuals on the spectrum from mistakenly thinking that meltdowns are "purposeful behavior" and to help them understand that unique responses to interventions are not "willful disobedience."

SELF-REGULATION AND THE BRAIN

Richey and colleagues (2015) found less activity in the parts of the brain that regulate emotions of those on the spectrum than of neurotypicals. The circled areas in Figure 1.1, which represent a composite of brain scans, show the areas of the brain that are significantly less active in people with autism when emotion regulation is required. Thus, it appears that challenges in regulation are brain based – not purposeful behavior!

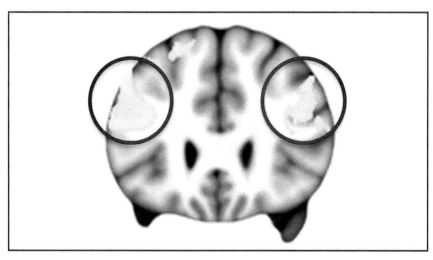

Figure 1.1. fMRI of the brain.

Adapted from "Neural Mechanisms of Emotion Regulation in Autism Spectrum Disorder," by J. A. Richey et al., 2015, *Journal of Autism and Developmental Disorders.* doi:10.1007/s10803-015-2359-z. Used with permission.

Judy Endow

When I am not well regulated, I am less able to engage in what is going on around me. It takes me much longer to process my thoughts. And, thus, my reaction time to the spoken words of others is much slower, and my reactions to extraneous stimuli become bigger and louder and last longer. I am told that my voice becomes louder and that I have a startle response to stimuli that normally would not cause me to startle. Until science advances enough to enable us to better understand and impact our neurological movement glitches – physical, thinking, and emotional fluidity – many of us with autism can learn to proactively outsmart at least some of the movement difficulties we experience by addressing our regulation needs.

Retrieved from www.judyendow.com

Lisa D.

Unlike temper tantrums, meltdowns are not manipulative tactics. Handling and preventing meltdowns is an important autistic life skill; and learning to predict them is a prerequisite to learning to prevent them. As we all probably already know, it's impossible to stop a meltdown once it happens – thus the focus on prevention.

Retrieved from www.judyendow.com

Leigh

Many autistic people are said to have difficulty understanding, labeling, and describing their feelings, but I've always considered myself to be quite lucky in this respect – I've always thought I could describe how I felt, most of the time at least. So when Joanna (my co-admin on this site) asked me yesterday, "How do you know when you're happy," I blithely answered, "When I'm feeling cheerful … when I have that joie de vivre, that glow inside. When I'm glad to be alive." "Yes," she said. "But how does that actually feel?" And I was stumped. She explained that I'd answered a question about a feeling by just using other feelings to describe it, leaving her no wiser about my experience of happiness.

Retrieved from www.judyendow.com

SENSORY ISSUES AND THE BRAIN

Neurological research has also informed us that the autistic brain perceives sensory input differently than typically developing brains. For example, studies have reported challenges in the sensory systems related to the auditory (Green et al., 2013), tactile (Green et al., 2015), proprioception (Marko et al., 2015), and visual senses (Soulières et al., 2009), with the visual system touted as a strength. In addition, behavioral differences have been identified in the olfactory and gustatory senses (cf. Ashwin et al., 2014; Bennetto, Kuschner, & Hyman, 2007). Further, the "overload of sensations" reported by many adults on the spectrum (see below) has been supported in the neurological research (Green et al., 2015). However, some individuals with autism experience the opposite; that is, they fail to process certain sensations (Tomchek & Dunn, 2007).

Table1.1

Location and Functions of the Sensory Systems

System	Location	Function
Tactile (touch)	Skin – density of cell distribution varies throughout the body. Areas of greatest density include mouth, hands, and genitals.	Provides information about the environment and object qualities (touch, pressure, texture, hard, soft, sharp, dull, heat, cold, pain).
Vestibular (balance)	Inner ear – stimulated by head movements and input from other senses, especially visual.	Provides information about where our body is in space, and whether or not we or our surroundings are moving. Tells about speed and direction of movement.
Proprioception (body awareness)	Muscles and joints – activated by muscle contractions and movement.	Provides information about where a certain body part is and how it is moving.
Visual (sight)	Retina of the eye – stimulated by light.	Provides information about objects and persons. Helps us define boundaries as we move through time and space.
Auditory (hearing)	Inner ear – stimulated by air/sound waves.	Provides information about sounds in the environment (loud, soft, high, low, near, far).
Gustatory (taste)	Chemical receptors in the tongue – closely entwined with the olfactory (smell) system.	Provides information about different types of taste (sweet, sour, bitter, salty, spicy).
Olfactory (smell)	Chemical receptors in the nasal structure – closely associated with the gustatory system.	Provides information about different types of smell (musty, acrid, putrid, flowery, pungent).
Interoception (inside body)	Inside of your body – helps the body "feel" the internal state or conditions of the body.	Provides information such as pain, body temperature, itch, sexual arousal, hunger and thirst. It also helps bring in information regarding heart and breathing rates and when we need to use the bathroom.

From Myles, B. S., Mahler, K., & Robbins, L. A. (2014). *Sensory issues and high-functioning autism spectrum and related disorders: Practical solutions for making sense of the world (2nd ed.)* (p. 10). Shawnee Mission, KS: AAPC Publishing. Reprinted with permission.

While research reveals strengths in visual processing, neurological findings also indicate that individuals with ASD process the features of faces as objects "and less in terms of their human significance" (Koshino et al., 2008, p. 289).

Clearly, there are many complexities that remain to be understood, but in this context, one thing is clear: being overwhelmed by sensory input – sound, taste, smells, etc. – or being unaware of sensory stimuli in the environment can result in meltdowns.

Sophie

When I get sensory overload, it is like I have 100 buzzy bees in my head, and my head hurts a lot and feels like it will go "bang" like a balloon. It is the most uncomfortable thing ever!!! I have to try to bang my head on things to try to relieve the pressure in my head to stop the feeling. While I am experiencing sensory overload, I find it very hard to talk or make any sentences, as my speech just won't come out as I want it to, and I can't make the words make sense.

Retrieved from https://www.autismspeaks.org/blog/2015/01/21/nonverbal-adult-shares-her-feelings-sensory-overload

Cynthia

From what I understand, typical people have a sensory processing system that operates like a fancy shower head. They can adjust the temperature and pressure and how the water flows until it's just right. People with atypical sensory processing, on the other hand, have a fire hydrant valve where that shower head should be. We get lots of data, all at once, all the time. Adjusting the flow of data ranges from difficult to impossible to totally unpredictable.

Retrieved from www.judyendow.com

REINFORCEMENT AND THE BRAIN

Comparing the response to social and monetary rewards in the brains of individuals with ASD to those of typically developing individuals, Kohls et al. (2012) found a difference between the two groups with respect to both types of rewards. Specifically, in individuals with ASD, the reward center of the brain, known as the mesocorticolimbic reward center, was underactive.

These brain-based differences may mean that situations that provide adequate reinforcers meant for neurotypicals do not provide adequate reinforcement for those with ASD. It is easy to see how a lack of positive reinforcement for appropriate behavior might lead to the frustration and anxiety that set the meltdown cycle into motion.

Chloe Rothschild

Positive reinforcement is important to me as a young adult with autism. I work so hard each and every single day, trying my best and giving it my all. Even if my progress and milestones may be small or different than others', they still deserve to be noticed. Something like asking to take a break isn't easy for me to do, so when I do, praise and positive words of encouragement are helpful. I want my efforts to be noticed.

Personal communication (October 19, 2015)

CONTEXT AND THE BRAIN
With sincere gratitude and apologies to Peter Vermeulen

According to dictionary.com, *context* is the conditions and circumstances that are relevant to an event, fact, etc. How we interpret the world around us depends on context. For example, context helps us quickly recognize and identify situations and things in our environment and helps us to understand what is relevant. Context also provides predictability: It tells us what to expect.

In his review of neurological research and context for individuals on the spectrum, Vermeulen (2012) pointed out that everything is sensitive to context. "Nothing in the world has an absolute meaning. A bag of garbage is not always a bag of garbage. Sometimes it is art" (p. 16). How we interpret our boss' message depends on the situation; how we understand our mother's facial expression depends on the situation. Everything is based on context – emotion recognition, the perceptions of others, our statements and questions, and overall behavior.

For most people, context "just is." Neurotypical individuals automatically interpret context – usually within 200 milliseconds. In contrast, individuals with autism often must assemble situations and contexts in order to make sense of them (Vermeulen, 2012).

> *In the documentary film* Autimatically, *Michelle tells how she recognizes her living room. Contrary to people without autism, Michelle does not recognize her living room in the blink of an eye. She first sees totally separate things: a flower, a VCR, a TV, a figurine on the mantle, the CD rack, and so on. Only when she makes a conscious effort does she succeed in assembling all of these impressions into a living room. Michelle also immediately notices when something has changed in her living room, even if it is only a slight detail.* (Vermeulen, 2012, p. 57)

According to Vermeulen (2012), those on the spectrum "have a keen eye for details, but not for all details. They excel in details for which context does not play a role" (p. 101). This means that they must expend considerable energy on first identifying objects, situations, people, and so forth, in their environment in a rote manner, and then, *if they have been taught how to understand context,* attempt to make the information meaningful. For individuals with autism, this is a deliberate process. For those without autism, this is a split-second automatic task. How exhausting this must be for a person on spectrum! And can this lead to meltdowns? Yes!

How else does context relate to meltdowns? Interpretation without context can lead to misunderstandings, error, and frustration. Context blindness can lead to heightened stress and anxiety because of the likely occurrence of mistakes in understanding social interactions. Difficulties understanding context can also lead to an overreliance on predictability. Once an individual on the spectrum has interpreted one situation correctly, he tends to rely on that interpretation in other events even if the context is different.

CATATONIA AND THE BRAIN

Catatonia is a brain-based disorder of posture/movement, speech, mood, and behavior (Northoff, 2000). The latest edition of the *Diagnostic and Statistical Manual of Mental Disorders* (5th ed., American Psychiatric Association, 2013; DSM-5) includes catatonia as a specifier for ASD. Indeed, approximately 12-18% of young people with ASD demonstrate some symptoms of catatonia (Billstedt, Gillberg, & Gillberg, 2005; Ghaziuddin, Dhossche, & Marcotte, 2012).

Catatonia has many complex (and frankly confusing) presentations. Some overlap with the underlying characteristics of ASD. When catatonia is present in somebody with ASD, they may have difficulty starting a motion, such as following directions or drinking when thirsty. They may also have difficulty stopping a motion. They may kick or hit someone when it is actually the opposite of what they intended to do.

The presence of catatonia is stressful and confusing both for those with ASD and those in their environment. Clearly, such stress along with the characteristics of catatonia and movement challenges increases the risk of meltdowns.

Judy Endow

When I am not well regulated, I also have significantly more movement issues. I must bring conscious thought to my physical movement, such as walking, grasping, and chewing. It becomes difficult to engage in multiple movements at the same time, such as walking over to a person and handing him something. First, I have to walk over to the person, stop, and then execute the handing-something motion. It also becomes difficult to combine physical movement with thinking. This means that I have to stop moving in order to think any thoughts unrelated to the actual act of moving my body through space. As a result, it is nearly impossible for me to walk and talk at the same time.

Retrieved from http://www.judyendow.com/autistic-behavior/autism-sensory-regulation-and-movement-fluidity/

SUMMARY

We are still in the genesis of understanding autism. In recent years, brain-based research and the perspectives of individuals with HF-ASD themselves have greatly contributed to our understanding, especially in the areas of meltdowns and other issues of regulation. Knowledge of the neurological underpinnings of ASD may lead to more patient and therapeutic responses to difficulties with regulation and a decreased tendency to respond in a punitive or judgmental manner.

CHAPTER 2

The Cycle of Meltdowns

We all experience stress. Most of the time, our stress is minor and/or easily addressed. However, many individuals with high-functioning autism (HF-ASD) experience stress that is ongoing and of greater magnitude. And as a result, their stress can be debilitating.

Common stressors include:

- Sensory issues, such as loud sounds, sudden sounds, odors, lighting, bright colors, patterns, moving objects
- Lack of predictability
- Difficulty communicating wants, needs, or ideas
- Change of events, including being added, canceled, resequenced, shortened, lengthened
- Perfectionism/fear of making mistakes
- Losing a game
- Being unable to convince others that your way is the correct way
- Being timed on tasks
- Facing unresolved problems
- Breaking a rule
- Anticipation of any events that will negatively impact you, such as negative feedback, failing to meet a standard, disappointing someone
- Being mistreated or treated unkindly (e.g., sarcasm, bullying, being left out of an activity)

In addition to generally experiencing more frequent and more severe stress than others, when they are first becoming stressed, people with HF-ASD often do not indicate in ways that are meaningful to others that they are under stress or having difficulty coping. In fact, they themselves do not always know that they are near a stage of crisis. Quite often they just "tune out" or daydream, pace, laugh, or state in a monotone voice a seemingly benign phrase, such as "I don't know what to do." Since no or limited traditional expressions of emotion may be conveyed, these signs of stress often go unnoticed by others in the environment.

Therefore, when at a later point in time, the individual with HF-ASD engages in a verbally or physically "aggressive" event or shuts down, it seems to happen without provocation. This is often called a meltdown. The person may begin to scream, kick over a piece of furniture, or totally shut down. For those who are not familiar with the characteristics of ASD, there seems to be no predictability to this behavior; it just occurs.

Sometimes support personnel report that an individual with ASD is doing fine or managing at school or work. However, family members report that when she arrives home, she loses control. That is, she experiences a meltdown. It seems that many people with ASD use all their self-control to manage at school or work, and that once they get to a safe environment (e.g., home), they let go of some of the pressure that is bottled up within them. Thus, the meltdown can occur in a totally different place from where the stressor was originally encountered.

Although it may seem that way, meltdowns do not occur without warning! Rather, individuals with HF-ASD exhibit a pattern of behaviors that are precursors to a meltdown. Sometimes these behaviors are subtle. In fact, those who do not know the person with HF-ASD often report that a meltdown comes "out of nowhere." One teacher reported, "Susan was just sitting at her desk quietly. The next thing I know, she had a meltdown. She totally lost control, over-turned her desk, and began flailing her arms. I had no warning."

Without training and/or experience – that is, without knowing the connections between meltdowns and ASD – the neurotypical person observing a meltdown may draw uncharitable conclusions. As a result, meltdown behaviors may result in rejection, punishment, fear, or judgment.

The alternative perspective presented here, on the other hand, will lead to more preventive strategies being put in place and more supportive responses given when meltdowns occur. **This is the kind alternative to uncompassionate misperceptions and misguided responses.**

Without a clear understanding of meltdowns and the cycle by which they occur, it may indeed appear as if meltdowns occur without warning. This chapter explains the cycle of meltdowns and how it affects both individuals on the spectrum and others in their environment. For each stage, behaviors and interventions are outlined, including suggestions for using "teachable moments."

THE CYCLE OF MELTDOWNS

Because meltdowns occur for a reason, it is important to understand the underlying causes or antecedent – that is, the triggers. The cycle typically runs through three stages: **Rumbling, Rage,** and **Recovery** (adapted from Albert, 1989; Beck, 1985). These stages may be of variable length, with one stage lasting hours and another only a few minutes.

The three stages can be conceptualized using a normal curve as illustrated in Figure 2.1 (Buron, personal communication, 2003;

LaCava, personal communication, 2003). But, in fact, we are actually dealing with double curves. The outside curve shows the cycle the individual with HF-ASD progresses through when having a meltdown; the inside curve depicts the cycle experienced by the support person. Most people focus on the cycle experienced by the individual on the spectrum, and rightfully so. However, the stress experienced by the support person is a part of the interaction and must be addressed as well.

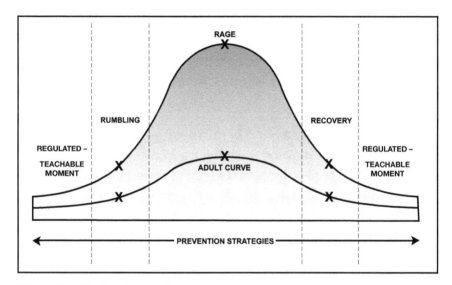

Figure 2.1. Cycle of meltdowns.
Adapted from Curtis and Dunn (personal communication, 2000).

Note the teachable moments at each end of the curve. These are the ONLY times when the individual with HF-ASD is available to learn new skills. That is, when she is in the Rumbling, Rage, or Recovery Stage, she cannot learn new skills but can only use skills that she already knows and is able to use fluently.

Learning can only occur when we are well regulated! This is important to recognize and respect. Failure to do so may escalate and prolong the cycle and cause additional frustration for both the individual with HF-ASD and the support person.

In the following, we will look at each of the three stages and present interventions that have been found to be effective for each.

Rumbling Stage

The first stage in the cycle is the Rumbling Stage.

"Behaviors" of the Individual

During the Rumbling Stage, individuals with HF-ASD exhibit specific behavioral changes that may not appear to be directly related to a meltdown. They may bite their nails or lips, lower their voices, tense their muscles, tap their foot, grimace, or otherwise indicate general discontent. In addition, they may appear to be slightly off-task, disengaged, or "off the mark." They may complain of not feeling well. It is easy for others to ignore these seemingly minor behaviors; yet, they often signal an impending crisis.

In other instances, individuals with HF-ASD engage in behaviors that are more pronounced, including withdrawing from others, either emotionally or physically; threatening others, either verbally or physically; or questioning the rules or authority.

Support Person Behaviors

As illustrated in Figure 2.1, as the behavior of the individual with HF-ASD escalates, the support person's behavior usually follows. Thus, those in a support role must realize that they may be experiencing their own rumbling behaviors along with the individual with HF-ASD.

Regardless of the specific intervention selected, certain general approaches are helpful when seeking to help the person who is rumbling.

During this stage, it is imperative that the support person remains calm and uses a quiet voice so he or she can focus on helping the individual move toward a more regulated state. It is almost impossible for the person with HF-ASD to be flexible unless he has been taught flexibility and it is firmly entrenched in his repertoire.

During this stage, the support person must be kind, reevaluate the goals, and be flexible so that the individual with HF-ASD can meet the "new" goal: **to get back to the teachable moment.** The behaviors shown in Table 2.1 are typically effective for those supporting an individual on the spectrum at this stage.

Table 2.1

Effective Support Person Behaviors During the Rumbling Stage

- Remain calm
- Use a quiet voice
- Take deep breaths
- Reevaluate student goals
- Be flexible – the individual on the spectrum is not able to

Just as it is important to understand support person behavior that may diffuse a crisis, it is important to recognize which support person behaviors are likely to result in an escalation. The behaviors listed in Table 2.2 are almost certain to turn a potential crisis into a meltdown (Albert, 1989).

Table 2.2

Support Person Behaviors That Can Escalate a Crisis

- Raising voice or yelling
- Making assumptions
- Preaching
- Backing the student into a corner
- Saying, "I'm the boss here"
- Pleading or bribing
- Insisting on having the last word
- Bringing up unrelated events
- Using tense body language
- Generalizing by making remarks such as, "You guys are all the same"
- Being sarcastic
- Attacking the individual's character
- Making unsubstantiated accusations
- Nagging
- Holding a grudge
- Acting superior
- Throwing a temper tantrum
- Using unwarranted physical force
- Mimicking the individual with HF-ASD
- Drawing unrelated persons into the conflict
- Making comparisons with the behavior of other people, etc.
- Insisting on being right
- Having a double standard: "Do what I say, not what I do"
- Commanding, demanding, dominating
- Rewarding the individual for unacceptable behavior
- Using degrading, insulting, humiliating, or embarrassing putdowns

Interventions

During the Rumbling Stage, it is imperative that the support person intervenes without becoming part of a struggle. Because many with HF-ASD do not recognize that they are under stress or are experiencing discomfort associated with the rumbling state (Barnhill et al., 2000), the help and insight of a support person can make the difference between escalation and resolution of a challenging experience.

Many effective interventions during this stage fall in the category of **surface behavior management** (Long, Morse, & Newman, 1976). This includes strategies such as antiseptic bouncing, proximity control, signal interference, and touch control. Strategies that do not fall under the category of surface management may also be used – strategies that are therapeutic, not punitive, and designed to support student success. These include cool zone/home base and "just walk and don't talk." Each of these strategies (see Table 2.3) will be briefly discussed.

Table 2.3

Rumbling Stage Interventions

- Antiseptic bouncing
- Proximity control
- Signal interference
- Touch control
- Defusing tension through humor
- Support from routine
- Interest boosting
- Cool zone/home base
- "Just walk and don't talk"

Antiseptic bouncing. Antiseptic bouncing involves removing somebody, in a nonpunitive fashion, from the environment in which she is experiencing difficulty. For example, in a school setting, Keisha is asked to take a note to the teacher across the hall. Jerome is asked to go to the art area to clean up supplies.

Similar interventions can be used at work. Andy, who recognizes and understands his rumbling behavior, is delivering a document to a colleague. Because he is "rumbling," he does not go directly from his office down the hall to his colleague. Rather, in order to become better regulated, he stops by the water cooler, goes to the supply room to get some new pens, and then heads to his destination. His way back to his office is equally circuitous. During this time, Andy has had an opportunity to regain a sense of calm so that when he returns to his office, the problem that prompted the rumbling has diminished in magnitude.

Proximity control. Rather than calling attention to somebody's behavior, when using this strategy, the support person moves near the individual who is engaged in "rumbling" behaviors. Often something as simple as standing next to somebody with HF-ASD is calming and can be easily accomplished without interrupting the event at hand or attracting unnecessary attention. For example, the teacher who circulates through the classroom during a lesson is using proximity control. A reassuring supervisor at the clothing store who moves near an employee when she is signaling "rumbling" by grimacing is also using proximity control.

Signal interference. When the person with HF-ASD begins to exhibit a seemingly minor precursor behavior, such as tapping his foot or clearing his throat, the support person gives a nonverbal signal – called signal interference – to let him know that she is aware of the situation. For example, she may place herself in a position from which she can make eye contact with the employee on the spectrum. To help the individual with ASD to recognize his or her own distress, a supervisor may use a "secret" signal as a cue.

Touch control. Sometimes a simple touch can serve to stop a rumbling behavior. Gently touching the arm or leg of a student who is tapping his feet loudly may stop the disruptive behavior.

Defusing tension through humor. This technique involves making a joke or humorous remark in a potentially tense moment. When using this approach, care must be taken to ensure that the individual with HF-ASD understands the humor and does not perceive himself as the target of a joke.

Some personnel are better at using this technique than others. Those who are not "gifted" in this area should not make this their first intervention choice during the Rumbling Stage, as misunderstood humor can lead to escalation to the Rage Stage.

Support from routine. Displaying a chart or visual schedule of expectations and events of the day can provide a sense of security and predictability, which is a central need for most individuals with HF-ASD. For example, the student who is signaling frustration by laughing may be directed to her schedule to make her aware that after she completes two more math problems, she gets to work on a topic of special interest with a peer. At work, a gentle reminder that a break will happen in five minutes can be helpful in keeping the employee regulated.

Interest boosting. Sometimes showing a personal interest in an individual with HF-ASD and his hobbies can help him to calm. This involves making him aware that you recognize his individual preferences. This also occurs when a task or assignment is shifted to include a special interest. Interest boosting can often stop rumbling behavior.

Cool zone/home base. Ethan and Amanda Lautenschlager (personal communication, 2004) created the term "cool zone" (which is synonymous with "home base") to describe a place where somebody can go when they feel a need to regain control. For example, a teacher might say, "McKenzie, when it is difficult to finish work, we use the cool zone to help students stay on track. Please take your work to the cool zone." He may then place an icon that says "cool zone" on McKenzie's desk.

The cool zone/home base is typically an environment that does not have a lot of traffic and noise but often contains calming items. For example, somebody who calms by rocking may use a rocking chair in the home base. Those who calm by drawing have access to art supplies.

Going to the cool zone does not mean escaping from work. In fact, work goes with the student, when possible. After the student calms through use of the calming activities in the cool zone, he then is able to do his work either in the cool zone or in the original environment if he is regulated enough to return.

School resource rooms or counselors' offices can serve as cool zones. Above all, whatever room is chosen, it must not be viewed as a reward or a disciplinary room, but should be seen as a place where the student can go to become better regulated. At home, a bedroom or den can be a cool zone or home base. At work, an office or break room can serve this function. Going to the cool zone can prevent the individual from progressing to the Rage Stage.

"Just walk and don't talk." Sometimes (unless the person is a "runner") an effective preventive strategy is to walk with the individual with HF-ASD. It is important here for the support person to resist talking because during the Rumbling Stage, the individual on the spectrum is beginning to feel overwhelmed. Any additional input simply adds to the feeling of being overwhelmed and will likely move him to the Rage Stage. In addition, even if the individual is able to process what is being said, anything the support person says is usually the "wrong" thing. The person on the spectrum is not thinking logically and will most likely react emotionally, misinterpreting any statement made by the support person or rephrasing it in such a way that its original intent is not recognizable. On this walk, the individual on the spectrum can say whatever he wishes without fear of discipline or logical argument. The support person should be calm, show as little reaction as possible, and never be confrontational (Jack Southwick, personal communication, 1999).

Summary

When selecting a technique for use during the Rumbling Stage, it is important to know the person with HF-ASD as the wrong strategy can escalate rather than de-escalate a situation. For example, touch control for some students appears to drain off frustration. That is, by merely touching the student's shoulder, the teacher feels an immediate relaxation on the part of the student. But another student might be startled by a touch because she (a) did not know the teacher was going to enter her space, (b) misperceived touch as an aggression, or (c) experienced touch as discomforting or painful due to sensory issues. In these cases, touch control would clearly have the opposite effect of the one intended.

Interventions at this stage do not require an extensive outlay of time, but it is important for those who wish to be supportive to watch for and understand the events that precipitate the target behaviors so they can (a) be ready to intervene early or (b) teach strategies to maintain regulation. Please note, however, that individuals with HF-ASD cannot be taught these strategies when they are in the Rumbling Stage! Interventions at this stage are merely band-aids. They do not teach ways to recognize or handle stress.

Rage Stage

If the rumbling behaviors do not stop, the individual with HF-ASD is likely to progress to the Rage Stage.

"Behaviors" of the Individual

At this point, the individual with HF-ASD is disinhibited and acts impulsively, emotionally, and sometimes explosively. Behaviors may include screaming, biting, hitting, kicking, destroying property, or self-injury. Another type of rage – internal rage – may also manifest.

When that is the case, the individual may completely withdraw, unable to verbalize or act in a rational manner (see Table 2.4).

Table 2.4

Typical Rage Behaviors

- Disinhibited
- Acting impulsively
- Emotional
- Explosive
- Destroying property
- Self-injurious
- Screaming
- Biting
- Hitting
- Kicking
- Experiencing internalizing behavior

Meltdowns are not purposeful, and once the Rage Stage begins, it most often must run its course. Adams (1997) related the following rage incident involving a young boy:

> *The first meltdown for one young man occurred while in a parking lot. A stranger swore at him and called him a "stupid kid." The boy started to shake a mailbox, and began to kick and scream ... It was noted by the parent that during later attacks, the boy would sometimes say, "I don't want to do this." It appeared that he could not disengage from the emotion, once it had started. (p. 72)*

Support Person's Behavior

When we find ourselves in situations considered very uncomfortable or dangerous, it is natural to react in a "flight-or-fight" mode. It is not uncommon for a support person to experience this reaction when working with an individual with HF-ASD who is in the Rage Stage. It is essential to remain calm – deep breathing can help attain and maintain this state. According to Hubbard (personal communication, 2004), the strategy "less is more" is also helpful for support persons to remember during this stage. In other words, the fewer words ... the better, and the fewer gestures ... the better.

Some people manifest rage by raising their voice or yelling. It is important that the support person not respond. Also, the support person should not take the individual's words personally. During this stage, the mouth of the individual with ASD is on "automatic pilot," saying words that are unplanned and not intended. Those in a support role should disengage emotionally by, for example, mentally creating a lesson plan, planning a grocery list, etc.

Generally, support persons should be nonconfrontational and use few words. Individuals at the Rage Stage are not thinking – they are reacting – so words have little meaning. As in the Rumbling Stage, it is important to reevaluate your goal for the person on the spectrum and be flexible. The ultimate goal at this stage is to move to the Recovery Stage. Table 2.5 lists a series of behaviors that are generally helpful for support persons during the Rage Stage.

Table 2.5

Effective Support Person Behaviors

- Control "flight-or-fight" tendency
- Remember that "less is more"
- Remain calm and quiet
- Do not take behaviors personally
- Disengage emotionally
- Be conscious of your nonverbal cues
- Take deep breaths

Interventions

Since no effective prevention can take place during this stage, emphasis should be placed on the safety of everyone in the environment as well as protection of property. The best way to cope with the rage is to get the individual to a cool zone, but only if she can be moved without physical assistance greater than a gentle touch.

Do not discipline or discuss discipline during the Rage Stage – or any other stage. As mentioned, the behavior is not purposeful or planned. Punishing during the Rage Stage would be similar to punishing someone for vomiting.

If the student has a meltdown in front of peers in a school setting, it is often easier to remove the other children. However, to do so, a plan must be in place, and assistance must be obtained to support the child or adolescent with HF-ASD or the other students during relocation.

Priority should be placed on helping the individual to regain control and preserving her dignity. Support persons should have developed plans for (a) obtaining assistance; (b) removing the individual from the environment or others from the area, as practical; or (c) providing therapeutic restraint, if necessary.

Interventions appropriate for use during the Rage Stage are listed in Table 2.6.

Table 2.6

Rage Stage Interventions

- Protect the student
- Protect the environment
- Protect others
- Don't discipline
- Remove any audience
- Be nonconfrontational
- Plan a "graceful" exit strategy
- Follow a plan
- Obtain assistance
- Prompt to a cool zone, as appropriate
- Use few words
- Prevent a power struggle
- Re-evaluate the student's goals
- Be flexible – the individual is not able to

Recovery Stage

Although many believe that the crisis cycle ends with the Rage Stage, this is not the case. As shown in Figure 2.1, there is a third stage: the Recovery Stage.

"Behaviors" of the Individual

Following the meltdown, the individual with HF-ASD may be contrite and apologize, often without full recall of the meltdown behavior. Or he may become sullen, withdraw, or deny that any inappropriate behavior occurred. Some are so physically exhausted after a meltdown that they just want to sleep (see Table 2.7).

Most often at this stage, the person on the spectrum is not ready to learn – he is not in a teachable moment. He is considered to be fragile. If not given significant time to calm down after the meltdown, some enter the cycle again and experience a shortened Rumbling Stage that quickly escalates to the Rage Stage.

Table 2.7

Typical Recovery Behavior

- Sleeping
- Denial of rage behaviors
- Withdrawal into fantasy
- Apologizing

Support Person's Behavior

Both the individual with HF-ASD and the support person experiencing the meltdown cycle are impacted. Thus, support persons must be aware that they also need to take time to recover. While it is often not possible for a support person to take time to relax and refocus immediately after the Rage Stage, it is important to schedule time for recovery at some point (see Table 2.8).

If the meltdown occurs at school, the teacher may attempt to relax in the teacher's lounge when her students go to music. At home, the father who was with the child during the meltdown may go out for a drive while the mother stays at home with the child. Perhaps after the child goes to bed, the mother who helped the child through the Rage and Recovery Stage can take a soothing bath. It is important that those who live or work with individuals with HF-ASD address their own needs in addition to the needs of others.

Table 2.8

Effective Adult Behavior During the Recovery Stage

- Remain calm and quiet
- Take time for yourself to regroup

Interventions

It is important that the support person works with the individual on the spectrum to help her to once again become a part of the routine or structure, as she is able. This may be accomplished in several ways, such as:

- Directing the individual to a highly motivating task
- Allowing the individual to work by herself
- Permitting the individual to be in close proximity to a support person
- Encouraging the individual to return to the daily routine with work that is at or below her skill level
- Having the individual use a relaxation strategy (only if it was previously learned and practiced during a teachable moment)

A rule of thumb for interventions during this stage is to use only interventions that are not cognitively draining and that the individual can perform with some degree of mastery. Skills may be considered mastered if they were taught, practiced, and mastered during teachable moments.

Some approaches are almost always counterproductive during the Recovery Stage.

1. This is *not* the time to discuss the rage behavior with the individual.

2. Do not attempt to teach a new strategy – whether at school or work.

A list of recovery interventions is presented in Table 2.9. These strategies are not intended to reward "bad"(!) behavior. Rather, they are intended to help the individual to return to the "teachable moment."

Table 2.9

Recovery Stage Interventions

- Allow the individual to sleep, if necessary
- Support use of relaxation techniques
- Do not refer to the rage behavior
- Support with structure
- Consider the individual to be "fragile"
- Plan instructional interventions to provide alternatives to tantrums, rage, meltdowns, and shutdowns
- Determine appropriate options:
  - Redirect to successful activity or special interest
  - Provide space
  - Ensure that interventions are presented at or below the individual's functioning level
- Check to see if the individual is ready to learn/go back to work
- Do not make excessive demands

Student Crisis Plan Sheet

The Student Crisis Plan Sheet (see Appendix) can be a useful tool in specifically outlining student behaviors and needed interventions for each stage in the cycle of meltdowns. This form helps educators and parents (a) develop a blueprint of events that are likely to precipitate meltdowns, (b) identify behaviors the student exhibits at each stage of the cycle, and (c) outline interventions that can be used at each stage to help the student regain behavioral control. The form is also helpful in ensuring that everyone involved is following that same plan to help the student exert positive control over her environment.

Regulated: Teachable Moments

A primary goal when working with those with HF-ASD who experience the meltdown cycle is to help them learn how to remain regulated. This can happen by:

- teaching them to understand their environment and themselves
- structuring the environment for success
- teaching skills that support academic, social, sensory, and behavioral success

When the Rumbling Stage begins, the support person must recognize the rumbling behaviors and initially intervene to help the individual with HF-ASD return to the teachable moment. However, they must also teach the individual to recognize in himself the rumbling behaviors and what he can do to move himself to a teachable moment. This generally takes considerable time and effort. Information about interventions that can prevent meltdowns is presented in Chapter 4.

The ONLY time an individual can learn a skill – whether academic, social, behavioral, or sensory – is during a teachable moment. Thus, considerable effort must be placed on *preventing* the occurrence of meltdowns so the individual on the spectrum is available to learn.

SUMMARY

To effectively carry out individualized interventions, we must analyze the behaviors that precede challenging situations, as well as those that happen during and after. Instead of random, hit-or-miss efforts, support persons have at their disposal a series of tools whereby they can more closely pinpoint behaviors and their causes. In the following chapter, we will look at a functional behavior assessment (FBA) as a means of accomplishing this critical task.

Overview of Functional Behavior Assessment

> *... the core of autism is sometimes missed, due to a tendency to focus too much on the behavior of people with autism (often even details of that behavior) without sufficiently taking into account the context of what is taking place in the mind of people with autism.* (Vermeulen, 2012, p. 353)

In the previous chapter, we discussed the immediate interventions that are helpful in responding to somebody on the spectrum who is in the *middle* of the meltdown cycle: Rumbling, Rage, and Recovery. However, it is also important to be knowledgeable about strategies that minimize or prevent the occurrence of meltdowns in the first place.

To prevent the cycle of meltdowns, it is important to understand the function(s) or purpose(s) of the behavior(s) exhibited during Rumbling, Rage, and Recovery. This process is known as functional behavior assessment (FBA). FBA is designed to answer the question, "Why does Johnny _____?" As such, it is a first step in developing effective interventions. Indeed, without determining the reasons, causes, or conditions under which a behavior occurs, interventions are not likely to be effective.

The following six steps comprise a functional behavior assessment and the resulting behavior intervention plan (FBA/BIP):

1. Identify and describe behavior.
2. Describe setting demands and antecedents.
3. Collect baseline data and/or work samples.
4. Complete functional analysis measures and develop a hypothesis.
5. Develop and implement a behavioral intervention plan.
6. Collect data and follow up to analyze the effectiveness of the plan (Aspy, Grossman, Myles, & Henry, 2016).

While an in-depth discussion of how to conduct an FBA is beyond the scope of this book, in the following we provide an overview of how to adapt the FBA/BIP process to address the underlying needs of individuals with HF-ASD – a critical and helpful process.

THE ICEBERG METAPHOR

Traditional FBAs are used to examine behavior as it relates to what occurs *before* (antecedents) and what occurs *after* (consequences) the behavior of interest. Traditional FBAs look at a limited number of functions: escape, avoidance, access to tangible or social reinforcement, and sensory stimulation. However, these functions are superficial because they do not address how the individual's autism impacts the behavior under scrutiny.

Schopler (1994) used an iceberg as a metaphor to illustrate the notion that visible behaviors (the portion of the iceberg above the surface of the water) are manifestations of underlying or "hidden" characteristics of ASD (the portion of the iceberg beneath the surface of the water). According to Schopler, effective behavior interventions must address underlying needs and not simply visible or "surface" behaviors (see Figure 3.1).

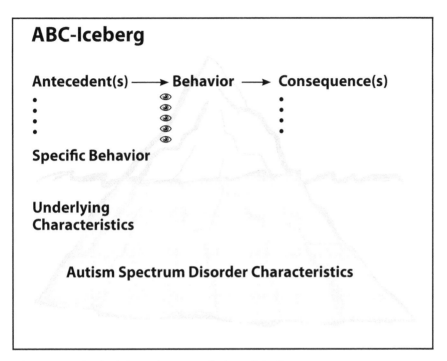

Figure 3.1. Underlying characteristics of ASD.

From Aspy, R., & Grossman, B. G. (2007). *The Ziggurat Model*. Shawnee Mission, KS: AAPC Publishing. Used with permission.

THE UNDERLYING CHARACTERISTICS OF ASD

Targeting underlying needs will lead to interventions that are more proactive and fundamental than those in a traditional FBA. By contrast, interventions that solely address surface behavior without consideration of the underlying ASD are potentially less effective and less likely to result in sustained behavior change. As illustrated by the Ziggurat Model (Aspy & Grossman, 2011), "Consideration of patterns of behavior in addition to underlying characteristics will lead to a better understanding of specific behavioral concerns and their unseen causes (p. 47).

The best way to understand a behavior is to look at the individual's ASD characteristics and how they are reflected in the behavior. The Underlying Characteristics Checklist (UCC; Aspy & Grossman, 2007, 2015) is designed to do just that. Alternatively, when working with a staff that is well trained and experienced in the area of ASD, the underlying characteristics may be identified from observations. Figure 3.2 shows the first page of the UCC – Adolescent Self-Report.

UCC-SR-ADOLESCENT
UNDERLYING CHARACTERISTICS CHECKLIST-ADOLESCENT SELF-REPORT
(12 to 18 years)

Ruth Aspy, PhD, and Barry G. Grossman, PhD, with Emma Goodall, PhD

NAME: ____________ **DATE:** ____________ **FOLLOW-UP DATE:** ____________

INSTRUCTIONS FOR COMPLETING INITIAL ASSESSMENT:
Each item describes behaviors or characteristics that may apply to you. Please place a check beside **ALL** items that currently apply. Use the Notes column to describe the behavior and characteristics in more detail, provide specific examples, or indicate frequency, settings, etc.

Projected **Follow-Up** date: ____________

Area	Item	✓	Notes	Follow-Up
SOCIAL	1. Have difficulty recognizing, understanding, or responding to the feelings of others			
	2. Have difficulty understanding what others may be thinking	✓	I often misread others and sometimes overreact because I thought that someone was being mean when they were not.	
	3. Stand too close to others (e.g., in conversation or in the hallway)	✓	People sometimes tell me that I bother them because I stand too close.	

INSTRUCTIONS FOR FOLLOW-UP ASSESSMENT:
Review checked and unchecked items. Use the Notes column to add further descriptors or to indicate changes. If an item no longer applies, strike through the check and explain changes in the Follow-Up column.

Area	Item	✓	Notes	Follow-Up
SOCIAL	1. Have difficulty recognizing, understanding, or responding to the feelings of others			
	2. Have difficulty understanding what others may be thinking	✓	I often misread others and sometimes overreact because I thought that someone was being mean when they were not.	Doing better at recognizing sarcasm
	3. Stand too close to others (e.g., in conversation or in the hallway)	✓	People sometimes tell me that I bother them because I stand too close.	

Figure 3.2. First page of the UCC-Adolescent Self-Report.

From Aspy, R., & Grossman, B. G. (2011). *The Ziggurat Model*. Shawnee Mission, KS: AAPC Publishing. Used with permission.

MIGUEL: CASE ILLUSTRATION

Miguel is a fourth-grade student who is being served in special education under the category of autism. Academically he is at or above grade level in all areas. Miguel is fascinated by the Revolutionary War and often reads college-level books about that period of U.S. history. Miguel enters the Rumbling Stage each time he is given an assignment from a new unit in the math book. His rumbling behaviors include talking to himself, rocking in his chair, and erasing his paper so hard that a hole starts to appear. He escalates to the Rage Stage by wadding up his paper, throwing it on the floor, and crying. He is reprimanded for his behavior and sent to the office if he does not calm immediately. In addition, his daily report to his parents documents loss of points for negative behavior.

Figure 3.3 shows an FBA-Iceberg (Aspy & Grossman, 2011) for Miguel completed through the use of a UCC.

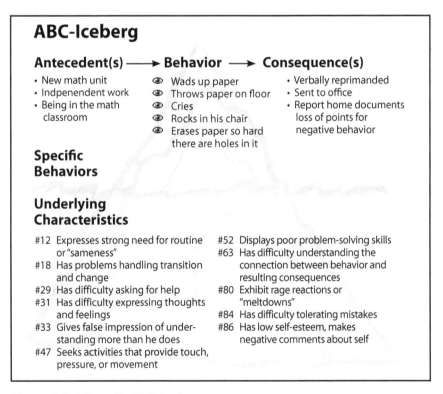

ABC-Iceberg

Antecedent(s) ⟶ Behavior ⟶ Consequence(s)

- New math unit
- Indpenendent work
- Being in the math classroom

- 👁 Wads up paper
- 👁 Throws paper on floor
- 👁 Cries
- 👁 Rocks in his chair
- 👁 Erases paper so hard there are holes in it

- Verbally reprimanded
- Sent to office
- Report home documents loss of points for negative behavior

Specific Behaviors

Underlying Characteristics

#12 Expresses strong need for routine or "sameness"
#18 Has problems handling transition and change
#29 Has difficulty asking for help
#31 Has difficulty expressing thoughts and feelings
#33 Gives false impression of understanding more than he does
#47 Seeks activities that provide touch, pressure, or movement

#52 Displays poor problem-solving skills
#63 Has difficulty understanding the connection between behavior and resulting consequences
#80 Exhibit rage reactions or "meltdowns"
#84 Has difficulty tolerating mistakes
#86 Has low self-esteem, makes negative comments about self

Figure 3.3. Miguel's ABC-Iceberg.

From Aspy, R., & Grossman, B. G. (2011). *The Ziggurat Model.* Shawnee Mission, KS: AAPC Publishing. Used with permission.

Once the UCC is completed, interventions are matched to each characteristic that is related to the behavior with a focus on comprehensive interventions. This occurs when each behavior is viewed from the lens of autism to address the five levels of the Ziggurat Model: Sensory Differences and Biological Needs, Reinforcement, Structure and Visual/Tactile Supports, Obstacle Removal, and Skills to Teach (see Table 3.1).

Table 3.1

Levels of the Ziggurat Model

Level	Description
Skills to Teach	Interventions that focus on teaching critical skills (often those that neurotypical peers learn without direct instruction).
Obstacle Removal	Interventions that involve changing the demands of a setting or task so that the individual with ASD is able to participate successfully.
Structure and Visual/Tactile Supports	Interventions related to routines and predictability as well as presentation of important information in a visual manner. *Note.* If the individual with HF-ASD has vision impairment, the supports would be tactile instead of visual.
Reinforcement	Preferred items or activities to increase the likelihood of positive behaviors.
Sensory and Biological	Interventions that address proprioceptive, vestibular, auditory, visual, olfactory, gustatory, interoception, and tactile, as well as supports for sleep, nutrition, and medical conditions.

Each of Miguel's underlying characteristics – salient to his target behavior – is then matched to interventions across the five levels of the Ziggurat Model (see Table 3.2).

Table 3.2

Miguel's UCC Items Matched to Interventions and Levels

Items from Miguel's UCC	Interventions* Based on Underlying Characteristics	Ziggurat Levels
• Expresses strong need for routine or "sameness" • Has problems handling transition and change • Gives false impression of understanding more than he does • Displays poor problem-solving skills • Exhibits rage reactions or "meltdowns" • Has difficulty tolerating mistakes	Use a visual calendar that shows when new units in math will begin	Structure and Visual/ Tactile Support
• Expresses strong need for routine or "sameness" • Has problems handling transition and change • Gives false impression of understanding more than he does • Displays poor problem-solving skills • Exhibits rage reactions or "meltdowns" • Has difficulty tolerating mistakes	Prime prior to new math units	Obstacle Removal
• Expresses strong need for routine or "sameness" • Has problems handling transition and change • Has difficulty expressing thoughts and feelings • Gives false impression of understanding more than he does • Displays poor problem-solving skills • Has difficulty understanding the connection between behavior and resulting consequences • Exhibits rage reactions or "meltdowns" • Has difficulty tolerating mistakes	Use a Stress Thermometer that indicates levels of stress and interventions that support each level	Structure and Visual/ Tactile Support

Table 3.2 (continued)		
• Has problems handling transition and change • Has difficulty expressing thoughts and feelings • Has difficulty understanding the connection between behavior and resulting consequences • Exhibits rage reactions or "meltdowns" • Has difficulty tolerating mistakes	Role-play using interventions on the Stress Thermometer to teach emotions and identify behaviors in self and interventions	Skills to Teach
• Expresses strong need for routine or "sameness" • Has problems handling transition and change • Has difficulty asking for help • Has difficulty expressing thoughts and feelings • Displays poor problem-solving skills • Has difficulty understanding the connection between behavior and resulting consequences • Exhibits rage reactions or "meltdowns"	Check-in to ask Miguel to point to his stress level on the Stress Thermometer	Obstacle Removal
• Expresses strong need for routine or "sameness" • Has difficulty expressing thoughts and feelings • Has difficulty understanding the connection between behavior and resulting consequences • Exhibits rage reactions or "meltdowns" • Has difficulty tolerating mistakes	Reinforce Miguel for pointing to stress level and using strategies	Rein-force-ment
• Has problems handling transition and change • Has difficulty expressing thoughts and feelings • Displays poor problem-solving skills • Has difficulty understanding the connection between behavior and resulting consequences • Exhibits rage reactions or "meltdowns" • Has difficulty tolerating mistakes • Has low self-esteem, makes negative comments about self	Use cartooning to illustrate the sequence of events as well as an alternative sequence of events when he uses calming strategies	Structure and Visual/Tactile Support

Table 3.2 (continued)

• Has difficulty asking for help • Displays poor problem-solving skills • Exhibits rage reactions or "meltdowns" • Has difficulty tolerating mistakes • Has low self-esteem, makes negative comments about self	Use nonverbal prompts to support Miguel in using the strategies	Structure and Visual/ Tactile Support
• Has problems handling transition and change • Has difficulty expressing thoughts and feelings • Displays poor problem-solving skills • Has difficulty understanding the connection between behavior and resulting consequences • Exhibits rage reactions or "meltdowns" • Has difficulty tolerating mistakes • Has low self-esteem, makes negative comments about self	Use cartooning to illustrate the sequence of events as well as an alternative sequence of events when he uses calming strategies	Structure and Visual/ Tactile Support
• Gives false impression of understanding more than he does • Exhibits rage reactions or "meltdowns" • Has difficulty tolerating mistakes • Has low self-esteem; makes negative comments about self	Reinforce use of math skills	Rein-force-ment
• Gives false impression of understanding more than he does • Displays poor problem-solving skills • Has difficulty understanding the connection between behavior and resulting consequences • Exhibits rage reactions or "meltdowns" • Has difficulty tolerating mistakes	Remove any competitive elements from math, such as timed assignments and sharing of grades	Obstacle Removal
• Displays poor problem-solving skills • Exhibits rage reactions or "meltdowns" • Has difficulty tolerating mistakes • Has low self-esteem, makes negative comments about self	Review past "new units" with Miguel to illustrate that he can do math and that "new units" become mastered skills	Skills to Teach

Table 3.2 (continued)		
• Seeks activities that provide touch, pressure, or movement • Exhibits rage reactions or "meltdowns"	Use thera-bands™ to provide Miguel with touch and pressure or allow Miguel to sit on a therapy ball, as recommended by the occupational therapist (OT)	Sensory and Biological
• Seeks activities that provide touch, pressure, or movement • Exhibits rage reactions or "meltdowns"	Ensure that Miguel's sensory interventions recommended by the OT are followed in the math room	Sensory and Biological
• Has difficulty understanding the connection between behavior and resulting consequences • Exhibits rage reactions or "meltdowns" • Has low self-esteem; makes negative comments about self	After he has completed a math assignment, permit Miguel to share a Revolutionary War fact with the class	Rein-force-ment

See Chapter 4 for more details about interventions.

Each of the levels is essential and contributes to the effectiveness of the others. Thus, if an individual's needs on *all* levels are not addressed, the intervention will not be as effective and skills will not develop.

SUMMARY

The traditional FBA, which focuses on antecedents, behaviors, and consequences (A-B-C), results in interventions directly linked to those three areas. The Ziggurat FBA-Iceberg presented in this chapter goes one step further by considering the relationship between an individual's autism and the target behavior. As such, interventions are directly targeted to the underlying characteristics, not strictly to the surface behaviors and, therefore, result in more meaningful change across environments.

A comparison of Miguel's interventions using a traditional A-B-C and interventions using the more comprehensive FBA-Iceberg is presented in Table 3.3.

Table 3.3

Interventions Based on Antecedents-Behaviors-Consequences vs. Those Based on Underlying Characteristics

Interventions Based on A-B-C	Interventions* Based on Underlying Characteristics
Provide "double points" for Miguel when he begins a new math unit	Provide visual calendar that shows when new units in math will begin
Send home report of Miguel's behavior, both positive and negative	Engage in priming prior to new math units
Give Miguel fewer math problems	Use Stress Thermometer that indicates levels of stress and interventions that support each level
Have Miguel begin new units in the resource room	Role-play using interventions on the Stress Thermometer to teach emotions and identify behaviors in self and interventions
	Check in, asking Miguel to point to his stress level on the Stress Thermometer
	Reinforce Miguel for pointing to stress level and using strategies
	Use nonverbal prompts to support Miguel in using the strategies
	Use cartooning to illustrate the sequence of events as well as an alternative sequence of events when he uses calming strategies
	Reinforce use of math skills
	Remove any competitive elements from math, such as timed assignments and sharing grades
	Review past "new units" with Miguel to illustrate that he can do math and that "new units" become mastered skills

Table 3.3 (continued)	
	Use thera-bands™ to provide Miguel with touch and pressure or allow Miguel to sit on a therapy ball, as recommended by the OT
	Ensure that Miguel's sensory interventions recommended by the OT are followed in the math room
	After he has completed a math assignment, permit Miguel to share a Revolutionary War fact with the class

See Chapter 4 for more details about interventions.

Which of the two types of interventions is more likely to meet Miguel's needs and lead to ongoing behavior change and skill development? The FBA Iceberg! Miguel's underlying characteristics listed on the FBA-Iceberg were selected because of the relationship between the specific UCC items and his behavior of concern. They directly address Miguel's autism and go beyond one situation in which he is experiencing difficulty.

Most individuals with HF-ASD demonstrate differences in multiple areas: social, interests, communication, sensory, cognitive, motor, and emotional. These differences, which are very real but sometimes difficult for others to see and understand, often make what seem to be routine events especially challenging.

Some individuals with HF-ASD have developed coping and calming strategies that allow them to spend most of their time in a regulated state; however, because of the ongoing challenges that HF-ASD characteristics present, many individuals with HF-ASD spend significant portions of their lives in the Rumbling Stage. Strategies that help a person to transition from the Rumbling Stage to the Regulated: Teachable Moments Stage may be needed on a daily basis in order to stay out of crisis – able to learn and participate within school, work, or community environments. Such strategies are presented in the following chapter.

Strategies That Promote Regulation

Individuals with high-functioning autism spectrum disorder (HF-ASD) do not want to engage in meltdowns. But for most, the meltdown cycle is the only way they have available to them to express stress, anxiety, problems with coping, or a host of other emotions and situations to which they see no immediate solution. This chapter discusses interventions that have been found to be effective for minimizing or eliminating meltdowns.

The best intervention for meltdowns is to teach skills to prevent their occurrence. However, as mentioned in Chapter 2, prevention strategies are effective only when the individual is not embroiled in the cycle of meltdowns. Teachable moments are exclusive to times when the individual is calm, focused, and relaxed (see Figure 2.1).

In order to break the meltdown cycle, it is important to support the development and use of skills and social understanding – the absence of which can lead to meltdowns.

Note. Many of the interventions described in this chapter fit into more than one of the four categories defined below. For example, social narratives can serve as both an instructional and an interpretive tool.

INSTRUCTION

To ensure appropriate and effective instruction of self-regulation skills, it is necessary to identify which skills are present and where skills break down in the face of daily demands. A common error in working with individuals with HF-ASD is to become blinded by their strengths.

▶ The fact that somebody can identify expressions of emotions in pictures does not mean that he can identify the same emotions in a real-life interaction.

▶ Even if someone can list the four steps to problem solving, that does not mean that she can independently utilize the steps when faced with a challenge.

▶ An individual who can list and describe the battles of the Revolutionary War may not be able to transition to a new math unit without becoming overwhelmed by the change.

Individuals with HF-ASD demonstrate many challenges and differences that require instruction to ensure they acquire skills that facilitate self-regulation – the major focus of this chapter. Most often, they do not automatically acquire many of skills that are otherwise taken for granted without a planned instructional sequence. An absence of these skills may lead to becoming overwhelmed and entering the cycle of meltdowns.

The following interventions will be discussed: (a) scope and sequence, (b) direct instruction, (c) social narratives, (d) hidden curriculum, (e) acting lessons, (f) self-esteem building, and (g) multimedia lessons.

Scope and Sequence

It is important to observe and carefully consider how somebody functions during actual tasks in real-life environments in order to accurately figure out her skill level. A range of task demands must be analyzed – noise level, age of others in environment, number of people in environment, availability of visual supports, length of task, time of day, temperature, and an infinite list of other factors.

A scope-and-sequence chart, such as the one presented in Figure 4.1, is helpful for identifying skill gaps or deficits. Once the task demands have been analyzed and the skill areas are identified, direct instruction to teach those skills may be provided.

Fundamental Skills	Making a complaint	**Getting Along With**
Eye contact	Offering an opinion	**Others**
Correct facial expression	Expressing basic feelings	Taking turns
Correct voice volume	Expressing complex	Sharing
Correct voice tone	feelings	Playing by the rules
Correct timing		Apologizing
	Social Response Skills	Being fair
Social Initiation Skills	Responding to greetings	Being a good sport
Using person's name	Responding to	Using kind talk
Using farewells	compliments	Being flexible
Greeting	Listening	Asking permission
Introducing self	Following directions	Cooperating
Asking for help	Making short comments	Dealing with "no"
Giving a compliment	Staying on topic	Compromising
Starting a conversation	Waiting	Dealing with a problem
Joining a conversation	Staying on task	Receiving a suggestion
Ending a conversation	Offering help	Giving a suggestion
Exchanging conversation	Giving encouragement	Letting others talk
Inviting someone to play	Reading body language	Showing interest in others
Introducing others	Reading the feelings of	Using humor
Joining in	others	Disagreeing politely
Talking about self	Dealing with mistakes	Dealing with teasing
Asking appropriate	Dealing with anger	
questions	Refusing when appropriate	

Figure 4.1. Sample items from a scope-and-sequence chart.

From Coucouvanis, J. (2005). *Super skills: A social skills group program for children with Asperger syndrome, high-functioning autism and related skills*. Shawnee Mission, KS: AAPC Publishing. Used with permission.

Because individuals with HF-ASD have an uneven profile of social, behavioral, and communication skills, it is important to understand the sequence in which these skills develop. Without an understanding of scope and sequence, it is possible to overlook the fact that a person may be missing an important prerequisite skill that might make a more advanced skill become rote instead of a usable asset. For example, if a child does not understand that tone of voice, beyond the actual words used, communicates a message, teaching the more advanced skill of using a respectful tone of voice to adults has little or no meaning. If the individual learns by rote to use that tone of voice, she will probably not be able to generalize it. The following materials, developed for individuals on the spectrum, offer scope-and-sequence charts.

> ***Super Skills: A Social Skills Group Program for Children With Asperger Syndrome, High-Functioning Autism and Related Challenges*** by Coucouvanis (2005). After a very helpful overview of the major issues related to social skills group training for children and adolescents with ASD and other social cognitive deficits, this very practical resource presents a collection of 30 lessons grouped under four types of skills necessary for social success: fundamental skills, social initiation skills, getting along with others, and social response skills.

> ***Navigating the Social World: A Curriculum for Individuals With Asperger's Syndrome, High Functioning Autism, and Related Disabilities*** by McAfee (2002) contains a list of 20 social/emotional skills that address (a) recognizing and coping with one's emotions, (b) communication and social skills, (c) abstract thinking skills, and (d) behavior issues. This scope and sequence (and accompanying lessons) seems particularly appropriate for girls with HF-ASD and related challenges. That is not surprising, as this resource was developed by a mother, who is a pediatrician, for her daughter.

> ***Social Skills Training for Children and Adolescents With Asperger Syndrome and Other Social Communication Problems*** by Baker (2003) also offers a scope and sequence of 70 communication and

emotion management skills for children and adolescents with ASD and related exceptionalities. Supported by many years of use in a clinical setting, Baker's scope and sequence is accompanied by an easy-to-use assessment measure that can be used by parents and educators. His assessment is unique in that it not only assesses whether the individual has a given skill, but also how often she uses it.

Building Social Relationships 2 by Bellini (2016). This book provides a comprehensive five-step model for social and relationship development that includes assessing social functioning, distinguishing between skill acquisition and performance deficits, selecting intervention strategies, implementing intervention, and evaluating and monitoring progress.

Direct Instruction

Unlike most of their typically developing peers seem to, most individuals on the spectrum do not automatically develop the social and behavioral skills necessary to be successful in school, home, and the community. As a result, support persons must provide direct instruction on these skills using a consistent lesson plan format incorporating traditional as well as nontraditional curricula.

Lesson Plan

A lesson plan is an instructional sequence that facilitates skill acquisition, including (a) rationale, (b) presentation, (c) modeling, (d) verification, (e) evaluation, and (f) generalization. Each lesson should incorporate these six elements, as reviewed below.

Rationale. In order to learn, many with HF-ASD need to understand how or why concepts required for mastery are relevant. Thus, support persons must relate (a) why the information is useful, (b) how it can be used, and (c) where it fits with the knowledge the individual already possesses. The rationale should include a visual task analysis that illustrates all the components of the lesson, including the amount of time to be spent on the lesson and which activities to complete.

One helpful guideline in teaching new skills to individuals with HF-ASD is: **Never tell what to do without telling why.** Providing the reason for using a skill often adds information about what others in the environment may think or feel in response to specific behaviors. This rationale is important for individuals for whom some degree of mindblindness (Vermeulen, 2012) may be present. It also increases the likelihood that the skill will generalize.

Presentation. Once the rationale has been introduced, the support person works with the individual to identify goals for the content. Then, using a direct instructional format, including both visual and auditory stimuli, the content is taught. Information is broken down into small increments and then presented. This type of instruction is active, with the support person sharing information, asking questions, and providing corrective feedback. In other words, direct instruction does *not* mean presenting a worksheet with a model and telling the individual to follow the directions.

Modeling. During the modeling phase, the support person first obtains the individual's attention and shows her what the skill or strategy looks like when used. For example, the support person may demonstrate (a) how to make a 911 telephone call calmly, (b) how to enter a group discussion at work, or (c) how to breathe deeply and think about a special interest as a way to become self-regulated when overwhelmed. The emphasis should be placed on what to do instead of what not to do. This is particularly important as many with HF-ASD know what *not* to do but have little understanding of what is required of them.

Every direction is explicitly spelled out, preferably using a visual support (see pages 79-84). The support person cannot infer that the individual understands a concept or format just because it has been presented before. Anything that is merely implied will likely not be understood. Models should be presented frequently.

Verification. Verification means making certain that the individual is "with you" during instruction and understands the information presented. Throughout the lesson, the support person closely monitors the individual's emotional state. Because those on the spectrum may have a flat, even seemingly negative affect, it may be difficult to tell, for example, when they are stressed as a result of not understanding specific content. The support person must work with the individual to understand how he or she communicates emotional distress and meet his needs as necessary through additional instruction, modeling, or individual work sessions. Failure to engage the individual in this very important step can result in him "tuning out" or, worse yet, having a meltdown.

The individual with HF-ASD must be actively engaged throughout the instructional process. For example, he may be provided physical cues to attend to relevant stimuli and be asked questions frequently. Physical cues could take the form of the support person using proximity control or a prearranged signal, such as clearing the throat or placing a hand on the individual's shoulder (see Chapter 2).

For the person with HF-ASD who requires a long processing time, the support person might present questions far in advance of them being asked. In school, a support person might share a "secret signal" that alerts the student that a question is forthcoming. For example, a teacher might tell the student that she will only be asked a question when the teacher stands next to her. When using this strategy, the teacher initially asks the student questions to which the student already knows the answers. As the student becomes comfortable with the strategy and, thus, more confident, the teacher can introduce questions that are more difficult. (No one else in the class needs to know that the student and teacher have this agreement.)

Evaluation. Following instruction, both the support person and the individual on the spectrum must evaluate skill acquisition. They should employ a variety of methods, such as role-play and video modeling, to assess understanding and use of the skill, including self-evaluating skill use and setting goals for generalization and maintenance.

Generalization. Programming for generalization must be a part of every instructional sequence by arranging for opportunities for individuals with HF-ASD to use newly acquired skills throughout the day and in a variety of settings. Support persons should also observe the individual in less structured settings, such as in a restaurant, store, or movie theater, to determine whether the skill has truly been generalized. Finally, assistance from family members is invaluable for ensuring generalization. Specifically, they can set up and/or observe home- and community-based events in which the individual with HF-ASD would be expected to use the skills.

Traditional Curricula

Several traditional curricula (that is, curricula designed for those with ASD for use by educational professionals, support persons, and clinicians) may be used to provide direct instruction.

> ***Social Skills Training for Children and Adolescents With Asperger Syndrome and Social-Communication Problems*** by Baker (2003) is structured so that educational professionals can plan a lesson in approximately 15 minutes. Each lesson includes a handout that summarizes the lesson and practice opportunities that can be given to parents, general education teachers, occupational therapists, and others who work and/or live with the individual with HF-ASD.

> ***Let's Talk Emotions: Helping Children With Social Cognitive Deficits, Including AS, HFA, and NVLD, Learn to Understand and Express Empathy and Emotions*** by Cardon (2004) offers a collec-

tion of easy-to-use activities on emotions for children ages 4-18. Children learn to identify and respond to their own feelings as well as the feelings of others.

Destination Friendship by Benton, Hollis, Mahler, and Womer (2011) was written by a team consisting of two special educators, a speech-language pathologist, and an occupational therapist, to provide easy-to-use, research-based strategies and activities that support the development of friendship skills for individuals with ASD within an active and fun learning environment. From the initial session, participants learn that what they say and do has a direct impact on others. Adult Tour Guides act as a personal GPS system by offering subtle coaching and social scripting through-out theme-based sessions that include social activities and situations in which children have immediate opportunities to practice their friendship skills. The Friendship Skills Checklist, a valuable tool included in this book, enables the user to identify the strengths and needs of individuals with ASD, resulting in a comprehensive assessment and interest inventory that can be used to guide social instruction and support.

Navigating the Social World: A Curriculum for Individuals With Asperger's Syndrome, High Functioning Autism, and Related Disorders by McAfee (2002) is a user-friendly program addressing social and emotional challenges.

Peer Play and the Autism Spectrum: The Art of Guiding Children's Socialization and Imagination by Wolfberg (2003) teaches adults how to set up play groups with typical peers and children on the autism spectrum. Everything needed to set up and carry out play groups is included.

Thinking About YOU, Thinking About ME – Philosophy and Strategies to Further Develop Perspective Taking and Communicative Abilities for Persons With Social Cognitive Deficits by Winner (2002) discusses perspective taking and comprehending academic activities that have social implications. Practical ideas, strategies, worksheets, and ready-to-use IEP goals are included.

Nontraditional Curricula

Social skills lessons can be supplemented with other materials that were not specifically designed for school use. The following is a brief list of books that may be used to teach social skills.

The American Girl series by Pleasant Company. Pleasant Company has published a series of books that are invaluable to girls of all ages. The books feature lifelike, attractive illustrations and use language that is informal, but informative. Books in the series include *The Care and Keeping of You: The Body Book for Younger Girls (*Schaefer & Masse, 2012); *I Can Do Anything: Smart Cards for Strong Girls* (Kauchak, 2002); *Writing Smarts: A Girl's Guide to Writing Great Poetry, Stories, School Reports, and More!* (Madden, 2002); *The Feelings Book: The Care and Keeping of Your Emotions* (Madison & Masse, 2013); and *A Smart Girl's Guide: Staying Home Alone: A Girl's Guide to Feeling Safe and Having Fun* (Raymer, 2015).

Social Rules for Kids: The Top 100 Social Rules Kids Need to Succeed (Diamond, 2011). This valuable resource helps open the door of communication between parent and child by addressing 100 social rules for home, school, and the community. Using simple, easy-to-follow rules covering topics such as body language, manners, feelings and more, this book aims to make students' lives easier and more successful by outlining specific ways to interact with others on a daily basis.

As a Gentleman Would Say: Responses to Life's Important and Sometimes Awkward Situations (Bridges & Curtis, 2012). Although this book is directed toward men (and male adolescents), it applies almost equally to women (and female adolescents). The book begins with 53 Things Every Well-Spoken Gentleman Knows, including how to listen, how to ask for favors, and understanding the meaning of "no." It also covers a diverse range of items related to lending and borrowing, dining out, meeting new people, and funeral behavior protocol.

How Rude! The Teenager's Guide to Good Manners, Proper Behavior, and Not Grossing People Out *(Packer, 2014).* This book covers everything from getting along with peers to using "neti-quette" (online etiquette). The book is fast-paced, entertaining, and written in teen-friendly language.

How to Behave: A Guide to Modern Manners for the Socially Challenged *(Tiger, 2003).* Designed for older adolescents and adults, this book covers travel by planes, trains, and automobiles; big-city living; leisure time; dating and love; and out on the town. It addresses issues that we often encounter, but with which few of us are prepared to deal, including lane blocking, tailgating, cutting others off, blocking, and merging when driving.

The Secret Rules of Social Networking (Klipper & Shapiro-Rieser, 2015). This book outlines the unstated rules that guide relation-ships overall. The book also demonstrates how one can carry these relationships into an online environment. The authors address Internet safety, romantic relationships, online vs. in-person interac-tions and more, with a particular focus on adolescents and young adults with communication and social skills challenges.

Life Lists for Teens (Espeland, 2003). This book is a great resource for teens of all ages. It covers an extensive array of topics about life experiences, and how to get along, learn, and have fun.

A Little Book of Manners: Courtesy and Kindness for Young Ladies (Barnes, 1998). This colorful book features Aunt Evelyn and Emilie, a preteen, who discuss telephone, mealtime, party, play-time and visiting manners, among other topics. The book is struc-tured as a series of short vignettes that can be read by or to a child.

A Little Book of Manners for Boys (Barnes & Barnes, 2000). In this book, written for boys between the ages of 6 and 12, Coach Bob talks about being good sports, taking care of things, eating, and other important issues. Parents can read one item per day with/to a child and discuss it at the dinner table or at bedtime.

Social Narratives

Social narratives are brief written paragraphs that provide support and instruction for children and adolescents with HF-ASD by describing social cues and appropriate responses to social behavior and teaching new social skills. Written by educators or parents at the child's instructional level, and often using pictures or photographs to confirm the content, social narratives can promote self-awareness, self-calming, and self-management. Minimal guidelines exist for creating social narratives other than to ensure that the content matches the student's needs and takes the student's perspective into account (Myles, Trautman, & Schelvan, 2013).

Social narratives may either illuminate or celebrate a skill that was demonstrated well or describe a situation that is challenging. At least half of the narratives used with any given individual should be positive, celebration narratives. This helps to reinforce new skills and prevent students from ignoring or avoiding narratives simply because they tend to focus on previous struggles.

Table 4.1 provides a set of guidelines that may be used to structure a social narrative for an individual with HF-ASD.

Table 4.1

Guidelines for Constructing Social Narratives

1. **Identify a challenging situation, a problem behavior, or a skill that has been used successfully**. The first time that social narratives are used, it is important to highlight individual successes. A behavior addressed in a social narrative should result in (a) increased positive social interactions, (b) a safer environment, and/or (c) additional social learning opportunities. The behavior should be task-analyzed and based on the individual's current skills.

2. **Define target behavior or knowledge.** The individuals who plan and implement social narratives must clearly define the behavior or situation in a way that the individual with HF-ASD can understand.

3. **Write the social narrative**. The narrative should be written in accordance with the individual's comprehension skills, with vocabulary and print size individualized. The stories should be written in the first or third person and either in the present (to describe a situation as it occurs) or the future tense (to anticipate an upcoming event).

4. **Display the narrative in a way that is commensurate with the individual's functioning level.** Depending on the individual's processing ability, more than one sentence per page may result in an overload of information preventing him from comprehending. For some, up to three sentences per page is acceptable. Each sentence allows the individual to focus on and process a specific concept. Pictorial representations can enhance understanding of appropriate behavior, especially for those with limited reading skills. Sometimes the individual for whom the story is written provides the illustrations. Decisions about whether to use drawings, pictures, or icons should be made on an individual basis.

5. **Read the social narrative.** The teacher or person should read the social narrative as a consistent part of the daily schedule. Further, the individual who reads independently may read the social narrative to others so that all have a similar perspective of the targeted situation and corresponding appropriate behaviors.

6. **Review findings.** If desired changes fail to occur after the social narrative has been implemented for two weeks, the narrative and its implementation procedures should be reviewed.

7. **Program for maintenance and generalization.** After a behavior change has been established consistently, use of the social narrative may be faded. Fading may be accomplished by extending the time between readings or by placing additional responsibility on the individual on the spectrum for reading her own social narratives.

There are many types of social narratives: (a) descriptive stories, (b) scripts, (c) the Power Card Strategy, and (d) conversation starters, as described below.

Descriptive stories. A descriptive story explains a situation, usually from the point of view of the individual with ASD. Descriptive stories are generally short and are written at a level that the learner can easily understand. Many times, they include pictures that help explain the story.

One of the best ways to write a descriptive story is to use flexible words, such as "usually," "sometimes," "often," "may," and "most of the time." Individuals with HF-ASD are often very literal, so if a flexible word is not used, they may experience difficulty interpreting the story if the details of a situation do not completely match the narrative.

Each descriptive story is different depending on what is important for the individual with ASD to be successful. Descriptive stories may:

- Tell what the individual will see, smell, hear, or feel.
- Describe the sequence of activities.
- Tell what other people might be doing.
- Describe what the individual should do in the given situation.
- Encourage the individual to try to participate.
- Remind the individual of reinforcers that will be available at the end of the activity.
- Describe what others might think or feel.
- Describe what the individual might think or feel.
- Describe supports or help that the individual can receive in the activity.

A descriptive story about riding on the bus might begin with the phrase, "I rode on the bus to the zoo." The entire descriptive story follows.

I Rode on the Bus to the Zoo

I rode on the bus to the zoo. During most of the ride, I wore my headphones and listened to Beyonce. I felt happy when I got to the zoo. Ms. Tutu was proud of me and she said, "You did such a good job on the bus. Your headphones really helped you have a good bus ride." I am proud of myself.

The following is a descriptive story for an adolescent who became upset when the schedule changed.

When My Schedule Changes

Sometimes I get angry when schedules change. Teachers usually tell me before things change. Sometimes teachers cannot tell me before things change. I will try to ask a teacher what to do if I am confused about the new schedule. It will be easier for her to understand what I need if I am not crying or yelling. Schedules can be changed, and it is okay to follow a new schedule. When the schedule is changed, my teacher will be there to help me.

Social scripts. Social scripts provide ready-to-use language for specific events. They may be structured as conversation starters, scripted responses, or cues to change topic (cf. Ganz, Kaylor, Bourgeois, & Hadden, 2008; Smith & Jelen, 2010). For instance, an individual on the spectrum may practice a script that includes key questions that can help him to begin a conversation . For the person on the spectrum who has trouble spontaneously generating language, social scripts are effective because they help with language recall.

When designing social scripts, care should be taken to include "context-friendly language." That is, common jargon should be incorporated as well as the informal language style used by peers.

The following is a script for a school-age individual with HF-ASD.

Asking Questions in Class

If you want to ask questions in class, here are some words that you can use with your teacher:

1. *May I ask a question?*
2. *I have a question.*
3. *Would you please say that again?*

The next script was created for a young adult with HF-ASD who did not know what to say to a professor regarding the supports he needed at the university.

Requesting Supports at the University Level

Excuse me, my name is Frank Masters, and I am really enjoying your class. I have a disability and need some accommodations. I will be recording your lectures on my phone so that I can listen to them a couple of times to make sure that I can learn what you are teaching. Also, I need more time to take tests, so the Office of Exceptionalities has arranged for me to take your tests in the study lab. Mr. Johnson will email you to make these arrangements. I hope that this is okay.

Thank you. And again, I am really enjoying your class.

The Power Card Strategy. The Power Card Strategy is a visually-based technique that uses a person's special interest to facilitate understanding of social situations, routines, and the meaning of language (Campbell & Tincani, 2011; Gagnon & Myles, 2016). The intervention contains two components: a script and a Power Card. A support person writes a brief script at the individual's comprehension level detailing the problem situation or target behavior. The script includes a description of the behavior and a statement of how the individual's special interest/hero has addressed the same social challenge. The individual is encouraged to use the same strategy to address a specific situation.

The second component of the strategy, The Power Card, which is the size of a business card or trading card, contains a picture of the special interest and a summary of the solution. Portable to promote generalization, the Power Card may be carried or Velcroed® inside a book, notebook, or locker or kept in a wallet or billfold. Figure 4.1 provides a sample script and Power Card used to support a high school student with HF-ASD.

Kazuki Takahashi Initiates Conversations That Focus on Others' Interests

Kazuki Takahashi is interested in other people and has learned to talk about things they like. He knows that people like to hear their name, so whenever he greets them, he says their name and looks them in the eye. He usually makes a point of finding out and remembering what their special interest or hobby is so that he can bring it up in conversation. If the person does not seem very talkative, he will ask a question about their interest and then listen carefully to the reply. Mr. Takahashi will use a key word from the person's reply to make a positive comment.

Kazuki Takahashi knows that people like to talk about their interests. He wants youto use the four steps that will help you have good conversations:

1. Greet the person by name and look them in the eye.
2. Ask about their interest and wait for response.
3. Ask a question about their interest and listen for a key word in their reply.
4. Comment on the interest using the key word

Put this strategy to use and find out Kazuki's secret to enjoying conversations.

Kazuki Takahashi talks about other's interests

1. Greet the person by name.
2. Ask about their interest and wait.
3. Ask a question about their interest and listen for key word.
4. Comment using the key word.

Figure 4.2. Power Card an Un-Gi-Oh.

From "Power Cards to Improve Conversation Skills in Adolescents With Asperger Syndrome," by K. M. Davis, R T. Boon, D. F. Cihak, & C. Fore III, 2010, *Focus on Autism and Developmental Disorders, 25,* 12-22. Copyright 2010 by Sage. Used with permission.

Hidden Curriculum

Everyone knows that Mrs. Kristmann allows students to whisper in class as long as they get their work done, whereas Mrs. Rafik does not tolerate even the faintest level of noise in her class. Everyone knows that Howard Johnson, the floor supervisor, is a stickler for clocking in and out, so arrival at work and clocking in and out on time are absolutely essential.

Everyone knows the rules for a nice restaurant …

1. You call ahead for reservations.
2. Upon arrival, you give the host/hostess your name and wait to be seated.
3. A waiter delivers a menu to you and may place a napkin in your lap.
4. And so on.

… Everyone knows … except the individual with HF-ASD!

Every environment has a hidden curriculum – the unwritten rules – the dos and don'ts that are not spelled out but that everyone some-how knows (Bieber, 1994; Myles, Endow, & Mayfield, 2013; Myles & Kolar, 2013; Myles et al., 2013).

Consider the hidden curriculum associated with going to the library.

When a teenage girl goes to the library with her father, she is there to check out a book. She talks quietly to her father, selects a book, checks it out, and leaves. This is one hidden curriculum item for the library. However, there is another hidden curriculum item for the library.

When a teenage girl goes to the library with her friends, the cur-riculum is different. Chances are that she is not there just to check out a book but to socialize, and that she will not talk quietly, unless prompted to do so. The hidden curriculum of going to the library with friends is to socialize, have fun, and not be kicked out of the library.

Individuals with HF-ASD are at a disadvantage because they usually do not understand the hidden curriculum and, therefore, inadver-tently break the rules associated with it – and, as a result, either get in trouble, become ostracized, or are hurt by peers.

They require direct instruction. They need to be taught, for example, that some middle school students curse, but that most kids don't curse in front of an adult. Adults on the spectrum need to know that even though they do not personally like their boss, they always speak to her with respect. And so on.

Persons with HF-ASD also need to know (a) expectations, (b) pleasing behaviors, (c) whom to interact with and whom to stay away from, and (d) behaviors that attract negative or positive attention. Understanding the hidden curriculum can make a huge difference in the lives of those with HF-ASD – it can keep them out of trouble and help them make friends.

Temple Grandin, the internationally known author and speaker, developed her own set of rules to guide her social interactions and behavior in society. Many of them are from the hidden curriculum (see Table 4.2).

Table 4.2

Temple Grandin's Rule System to Guide Her Social Interactions and Behavior

1. **Really Bad Things** – Examples: murder, arson, stealing, lying in court under oath, injuring or hitting other people. All cultures have prohibitions against really bad things because an orderly, civilized society cannot function if people are robbing and killing each other.

2. **Courtesy Rules** – Do not cut in on a line at the movie theater or airport, observe table manners, say thank you, and keep yourself clean. These things are important because they make the other people around you more comfortable. I don't like it when somebody else has sloppy table manners, so I try to have decent table manners. It annoys me if somebody cuts in front of me in a line, so I do not do this to other people.

3. **Illegal But Not Bad** – Examples: slight speeding on the freeway and illegal parking. However, parking in a handicapped zone would be worse because it would violate the courtesy rules.

Table 4.2 (continued)

4. **Sins of the System (SOS)** – Examples: smoking pot (and being thrown in jail for ten years) and sexual misbehavior. SOSs are things where the penalty is so severe that it defies all logic. Sometimes, the penalty for sexual misbehavior is worse than killing somebody. Rules governing sexual behavior are so emotionally based that I do not dare discuss the subject for fear of committing an SOS. An SOS in one society may be acceptable behavior in another, whereas rules 1, 2, 3 tend to be more uniform between different cultures. I have never done a sin of the system ... People with autism have to learn that certain behaviors will not be tolerated – period. You will be fired no matter how good your work is if you commit an SOS at work. People with autism and Asperger's need to learn that if they want to keep a job, they must not commit an SOS ... The social knowledge required is just too complex.

Grandin, T. (1999, April). *Understanding people with autism: Developing a career makes life satisfying.* Paper presented at the MAAP Services, Incorporated (chart@netnitco.net), and Indiana Resource Center for Autism Conference, Indianapolis, IN. Used with permission of MAAP Services, Inc..

Who should teach the hidden curriculum? Anyone who supports the individual with HF-ASD. There are many hidden curriculum items, such as how to interact with other students and adults at school, that teachers can comfortably teach and should teach as they would reading, writing, or social studies. There are other hidden curriculum items, such as understanding the rules associated with dating and developing intimate relationships, about which peers and familiar adults should provide instruction. Table 4.3 provides a sample list of hidden curriculum items.

Table 4.3

Sample Hidden Curriculum Items

- Treat all authority figures with respect (e.g., police, firefighters). You would not address a police officer like you would your brother.
- Not all people you are unfamiliar with are strangers you cannot trust. You may not know your bus driver or your police officer, but these are people who help you.

Table 4.3 (continued)

- What may be acceptable at your house may not be acceptable at a friend's house. For example, although it is acceptable to put your feet up on the table at home, your friend's mom may be upset if you do that in their home.
- People do not always want to know the honest truth even when they ask. Your best friend does not want to hear that she looks fat in a new dress she just bought for special occasion.
- It is impolite to interrupt someone talking, unless it is an emergency.
- Acceptable slang that may be used with your peers (e.g., dawg, phat) may not be acceptable when interacting with adults.
- If you wish to keep your job, you must be nice to your boss or supervisor even if you do not like him or her.
- When a teacher tells another student to stop talking, it is not an appropriate time for you to start talking to your neighbor.

Myles, B. S., Trautman, M. L., & Schelvan, R. L. (2013). *The hidden curriculum: Practical solutions for understanding unstated rules in social situations* (2nd ed.). Shawnee Mission, KS: AAPC Publishing. Used with permission.

Acting Lessons

Many adults with HF-ASD suggest that acting lessons are an effective means of teaching self-regulation and social understanding. During acting lessons, they learn to express verbally and nonverbally their emotions in specific situations. They also learn to interpret others' emotions, feelings, and voices. Perhaps more important, in acting class participants engage in simulations and receive direct and immediate feedback from an instructor and peers regarding their performance.

One adult with AS, Margo, credits her success in expressing emotions and interpreting social situations to acting lessons. She acknowledges that her "real-life" performances may be a bit stilted, but after taking acting classes she understands better how to act and react in a neurotypical world.

Self-Esteem Building

Individuals with HF-ASD may look different, act different, feel different, and, in some ways, be different from others. They often know this, and, sadly, loss of self-esteem is frequently the by-product. For adults, sadly, there is a high price to pay for a negative self-esteem. It has been documented that adults with AS have higher levels of depression, anxiety, suicide, and other affective disorders than the general population, which can partially be related to their self-concept (cf. Moss, Howlin, Savage, Bolton, & Rutter, 2015).

Support persons must help those on the spectrum to understand that they are more than their exceptionality. They are not HF-ASD! Yes, they have an exceptionality, but this is only one part of them. They have many characteristics that must be pointed out and celebrated (cf. Kirchner & Dziobek, 2014; Winter-Messiers, 2007). Positive aspects of HF-ASD along with other strengths should be emphasized. The individual should understand that all people are special. Everyone is able to do certain things well, while other tasks are challenging. The following is a list of resources that reinforce the idea that individuals with HF-ASD have many strengths and unique talents.

> ***Genius Genes: How Asperger Challenges Changed the World***
> (2007) by Fitzgerald and O'Brien state that aspects of Asperger syndrome may be advantageous in evoking new thinking, creativity and inventiveness, and that this may be "the difference that makes all the difference" in terms of human evolution. Asperger syndrome is often portrayed as a negative phenomenon – a kind of affliction or curse – but if it was an integral part of the make-up and mindset of Newton, Darwin, and Einstein, arguably science's three most important personalities, it can clearly be seen in some respects as a gift to humanity. The authors further state that it may be no exaggeration to say that Asperger intelligence has shaped the world as we know it.

Neurotribes: The Legacy of Autism and the Future of Neurodiversity (2015a) by Silberman provides the first complete history of ASD and describes the movement among some individuals with HF-ASD called neurodiversity. These individuals seek "respect, support, technological innovation, accommodations in the workplace and in education, and the right to self-determination for those with cognitive differences" (Silberman, 2015b).

Uniquely Human: A Different Way of Seeing Autism by Prizant (2015) posits that instead of being seen as signs of pathology, "autistic" behaviors are part of a range of strategies designed to cope with an overwhelming world. As a result, rather than curbing these behaviors, as traditionally has been the focus of support and intervention, Prizant emphasizes that it is better to enhance abilities, build on strengths, and offer supports that will lead to a better quality of life.

In a Different Key: The Story of Autism by Donvan and Zucker (2016) tells the story of the first child diagnosed by Kanner and traces the history of autism highlighting the courageous people who helped the world understand the spectrum as well as the many the important events and controversies associated with the history of ASD.

Asperger's and Self-Esteem: Insight and Hope Through Famous Role Models by Ledgin (2002) takes a specific route to help individuals with HF-ASD develop positive self-esteem. Specifically, Ledgin identifies 13 adults who seem to share some of the characteristics of HF-ASD, including Charles Darwin, Orson Welles, Carl Sagan, Albert Einstein, and Marie Curie. Ledgin's message is that although individuals with HF-ASD have challenges, they can be very successful.

Multimedia Lessons

Most individuals with HF-ASD are visual learners, so interventions that use the visual modality are often especially effective. One such intervention is videos. In addition to their visual format, videos offer several advantages. For example, (a) they show skills in a fluid format so that they can be seen as a whole instead of as a set of discrete steps, (b) they are often motivating because of their pace and content, and (c) they allow for multiple viewings to ensure that learners acquire the skill that is targeted.

Four video-based strategies – video modeling, video detective, vintage videos, and commercial software – are discussed below.

Video modeling. Using video self-modeling, individuals learn to interact with others by observing themselves or others on videotape engaging in an interaction.

One type of video self-modeling is *positive self-review*. The individual is taped when engaging in a behavior, and the video is used as a reminder to engage in that behavior. Positive self-review is best employed when the learner has developed a specific social skill but is either (a) not using it at the appropriate level because it is newly acquired, or (b) not maintaining it in the natural environment (Acar & Diken, 2012).

Another type of video self-modeling is *feedforward*. This approach is used when somebody has learned individual skills but cannot put them together and use them in a real-life situation. In addition, it can assist in transferring skills across environments.

> *JaeWook had learned all the steps for approaching and talking with a colleague during lunch, but when given the opportunity to use these skills, he would freeze after merely saying hello. To help him use the skills, his job coach videotaped JaeWook engaging in the steps he had learned to use and edited the tape so that it showed all the individual steps sequentially. When JaeWook saw the videotape, he was able to transfer the interaction skills during lunch.*

Video detective. In another example of how to use videotapes, one mother teaches her son about nonverbal communication through the television series *Blue Bloods* and *The Big Bang Theory*. After she has introduced a concept, she plays the television show with the sound turned down and asks her son to predict the actors' nonverbal and verbal communication messages based on what he sees on the screen.

Similarly, a facilitator of an adult social skills group routinely videotapes participants during planned simulations and regular activities and uses the videos as instructional tools. This allows the adults on the spectrum to see themselves giving mixed messages or using effective verbal strategies to communicate to others, and also to monitor their voice tone or proximity. The facilitator also works with small groups to create scripts that the adults act out on video. She plays the videotaped scripts and hosts two game show-type activities for her contestants, "What's My Emotion?" and "Find the Conversation Flaw."

Vintage videos. Vintage videos can be excellent teaching tools. For example, silent Charlie Chaplin and Buster Keaton movies offer opportunities to view facial expressions and link them with situations without having to navigate through spoken language. Similarly, the character Lucy Ricardo of the television show *I Love Lucy* offers exaggerated facial expressions that can also be helpful in teaching social understanding.

Software. Authored by Simon Baron-Cohen (2007), *Mind Reading: The Interactive Guide to Emotions* software program teaches human emotions to individuals who experience difficulty in this area. Users can see and hear 400 different emotions expressed in people from different racial/ethnic groups across the lifespan. In addition, the software package contains an emotions library, a learning center with lessons and quizzes, and a game zone that allows practice in a video-game type format.

INTERPRETATION

Interpretation refers to the recognition that, no matter how well developed their skills, situations will arise that persons with HF-ASD do not understand. In addition to confusion, this may result in extreme stress, which may lead to the cycle of meltdowns, as discussed earlier. To help prevent this from happening, someone in the environment must serve as an interpreter using a variety of techniques to help to explain the social environment.

Interpretative strategies include (a) rating scales, (b) sensory aware-ness, (c) cartooning, and (d) social autopsies. We will discuss each option below.

Rating Scales

Behavior regulation includes the ability to read and self-monitor positive and negative reactions as well as to understand elements in the environment that may cause discomfort. As mentioned, individuals with HF-ASD often have difficulty interpreting their emotions and social well-being. This is not because they are avoiding an uncomfortable situation or misleading themselves or others, but because they often cannot tell what they are feeling. In addition, individuals with HF-ASD have difficulty self-calming (cf., Myles, Hagiwara et al., 2004; Myles, Mahler, & Robbins, 2014). Therefore, it is important to provide strategies that will help them to understand their emotions and to respond appropriately.

Two rating scales address this important topic.

Stress-tracking thermometer. McAfee's (2002) stress-tracking thermometer from *Navigating the Social World* works well with in-dividuals on the spectrum. Through the use of a Stress Thermome-ter, individuals with HF-ASD learn to:

- Identify and label their emotions using nonverbal and situational cues
- Assign appropriate values to different degrees of emotion, such as anger
- Redirect negative thoughts to positive thoughts
- Identify environmental stressors and common reactions to them
- Recognize the early signs of stress
- Select relaxation techniques that match their needs

A sample Stress Thermometer appears in Figure 4.3.

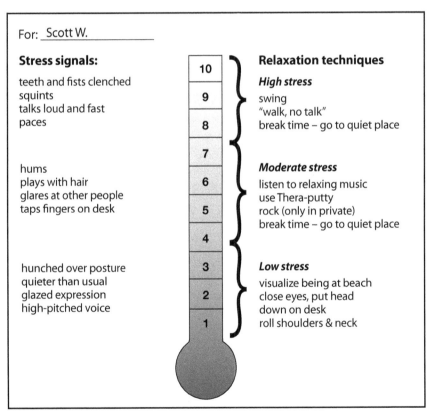

Figure 4.3. Stress Thermometer.

From McAfee, J. (2002). *Navigating the social world: A curriculum for individuals with Asperger's syndrome, high functioning autism and related disorders* (p. 47). Arlington, TX: Future Horizons, Inc. Reprinted with permission.

The Incredible 5-Point Scale. Incredible 5-Point Scale books have been developed to help children (Buron & Curtis, 2012) as well as adolescents and adults with AF-ASD (Buron, Brown, Curtis, & King, 2012) to understand themselves, and therefore, to be able to better regulate their behavior. The scale is unique in that it has a wide range of applications. For example, it can be used as an obsessional index, a stress scale, a meltdown monitor, and so on. Individuals on the spectrum learn to recognize the stages of their specific behavioral challenges and methods to self-calm at each level. The Incredible 5-Point Scale identifies, in the individual's own words, (a) a term to describe her behavior at a 1, 2, etc.; (b) what the behavior feels like at each number; and (c) what she can do to address the behavior at each level. Figures 4.4 and 4.5 provide illustrations of how the Incredible 5-Point Scale may be used.

The Obsessional Index

Kevin is in the fifth grade. He has ASD and obsessive compulsive disorder. Kevin is obsessed with balls and will go to great lengths to find a ball and then throw it on top of the highest available ledge or roof. The ball-throwing obsession becomes a problem when he hurts others to get at a ball or when he runs through the school with a ball trying to find a high ledge. His anxiety over ball throwing is so intense that his thinking becomes illogical.

The following is Kevin's account of his ball obsession, which he reported to his teacher when she interviewed him as a part of a functional behavior assessment:

"I don't want to be obsessed with balls or balloons. It is a stupid obsession. I can't be the boss of anything. I want to be back to being a baby again. Maybe then I could start over. When I go to people's houses, I steal their balls, and that's embarrassing. No one in the neighborhood understands me. I hate obsessions. They make me mad. I really want to get rid of them but I can't. I can't do anything right. Every time I see a ball, I have to have it. I know right from wrong but this is just too hard."

The 5-Point Scale was designed to teach Kevin how to recognize his need for support in dealing with his obsessions before it was too late. On some days, he didn't even seem to think about balls; in fact, on those days his obsessive personality seemed to help him to stay focused on his work. On other days, he would think about balls but it didn't seem to bother him much. On those days, he was so relaxed that he could handle thoughts about balls.

The Obsessional Index (continued)

Some days he just wanted to talk about his obsession with balls. If the adult with him told him not to talk about it, it often led to increased anxiety and acting-out behavior. Some days Kevin would come off the bus already talking rapidly about balls, types of balls, sizes of balls, and so on. We knew that on those days, he was going to need added support. This support often meant that Kevin did his work outside of the classroom to lower his anxiety about "blowing it" in front of the other kids.

Kevin had refused social stories in the past because he thought they were for "babies." Instead, we wrote him a memo to explain the new scale idea. Kevin loved the memo and kept it with him. He checked in with the special education teacher each morning to rate himself, and within a month he was accurately rating his anxiety about balls.

After we introduced the memo to him, there have only been a few days when Kevin had to work outside of the classroom for most of the day because his anxiety was high. Although he continues to have occasional rough days, he has not had to leave the classroom since we started the program.

MEMO

To: Kevin

Re: When Your Obsessions Get Too Big

Sometimes having obsessions can be a positive thing, because it means that your brain is capable of latching onto an idea and not letting go. This can be beneficial for great explorers, inventors and writers. BUT sometimes having obsessions can be very upsetting and frustrating.

This memo is to inform you that I understand that sometimes your obsessions get so big that you are not able to control them because of the severe level of anxiety they cause. It would be highly beneficial for you to learn to tell the difference between when your obsessions are too big to handle and when they are feeling more like positive obsessions. One way to do this is to do a "check-in" three times a day when you consider your obsessional index. The first step is to help me fill out the following chart by rating your obsessional index on a 1-5 rating scale. Thank you for your cooperation.

Kari Dunn Buron

Figure 4.4. The Incredible 5-Point Scale: Kevin's Obsessional Index.

From Buron, K. D., & Curtis, M. (2012). *The Incredible 5-Point Scale: The significantly improved and expanded second edition.* Shawnee Mission, KS: AAPC Publishing (pp. 17-18). Reprinted with permission.

"I'm 6'2", Strong as an Ox –
So Can You Tell Me Why I'm Trembling?"

David was referred to the self-contained high school program after being expelled from his home high school. He had broken several windows in the school cafeteria and the glass entrance/exit door nearest to the cafeteria. As a result, he had been to juvenile court and was placed on probation.

David identified his behavior as self-defense. "It was like my head was going to explode because of all the noise and confusion in the cafeteria. It's always confusing, and today there was a food fight. I had to do something to make it stop, I was afraid my head was going to explode."

The rating scale that follows does not rate David's level of anger, but his fear. David told us he feels afraid when he is "confused" so when developing this scale, we discussed things that we were afraid of, and David drew pictures to help him understand his own fear.

Understanding My Feelings
by David

Scared/Afraid

My word for this is:
trembling

This is how I look:

This is how my body feels:

This is what I do:
Hide.

This is what I say:
"I've got to get out of here!"

Things that David says make him "tremble":
"When I get confused."
"When it is loud and crowded."
"Catastrophes like tornadoes and earthquakes and war."

Name: _David_   My _scared/Afraid/Trembling_   Scale

Rating	Looks/sounds like	Feels like	Safe people can help/I can try to
5	Wide-eyed, maybe screaming, and running, hitting.	I am going to explode if I don't do something.	I will need an adult to help me leave. Help!
4	Threaten others or bump them.	People are talking about me. I feel irritated, mad.	Close my mouth and hum. Squeeze my hands. Leave the room for a walk.
3	You can't tell I'm scared. Jaw clenched.	I shiver inside.	Write or draw about it. Close my eyes.
2	I still look normal.	My stomach gets a little queasy.	Slow my breathing. Tell somebody safe how I feel.
1	Normal - you can't tell by looking at me.	I don't know, really.	Enjoy it!

Figure 4.5. The Incredible 5-Point Scale: Understanding my feelings.

From Buron, K. D., & Curtis, M. (2012). *The Incredible 5-Point Scale: The significantly improved and expanded second edition.* Shawnee Mission, KS: AAPC Publishing (pp. 39-41). Reprinted with permission.

Sensory Awareness

All of the information we receive from our environment comes through the sensory system. Taste, smell, sight, sound, touch, movement, the force of gravity, body position, and internal sensations are the basic sensory ingredients that enable all individuals to listen, attend for a period of time, and be calm enough or awake enough to participate in learning experiences and other daily activities (cf. Mahler, 2015; Myles et al., 2014).

Those who interact with individuals with HF-ASD often assume that they have an intact sensory system, but this is not always the case (Marco, Hinkley, Hill, & Nagarajan, 2011). In fact, individuals on the spectrum often have one or more areas of the sensory system that is oversensitive, undersensitive, or alternatively over- and undersensitive.

A sensory diet (Flanagan, 2016) is one way to provide sensory-based activities selected to address the specific needs of an individual (e.g., movement, touch, auditory). Activities are provided in a systematic, prescriptive manner (Case-Smith, Weaver, & Fristad, 2015). With the assistance of an occupational therapist who is knowledgeable about sensory functioning, individuals with HF-ASD can be taught how to recognize their sensory differences and to incorporate sensory strategies into their daily activities to help them to remain regulated and reduce the risk of entering the cycle of meltdowns.

Cartooning

Visual symbols, such as schedules and cartoons, have been found to enhance an understanding of the environment. For example, research has shown that visual support can serve as an effective means of teaching educational, functional living, and social skills (cf. Lequia, Machalicek, & Rispoli, 2012).

One type of visual support is cartooning. The technique of cartooning, used as a generic term, has been implemented by speech-language pathologists for many years to enhance their clients' understanding, including illustrating the meaning of idioms, understanding the sequence of events, and interpreting social situations. Used in more specific ways, cartooning has played an integral role in several intervention techniques such as pragmaticism (Arwood & Kaulitz, 2007) and Comic Strip Conversations™ (Gray, 1994).

Cartooning promotes social understanding by incorporating simple figures and other symbols in a comic strip format. Speech, thought bubble symbols, and sometimes color are used to help the individual with HF-ASD see and analyze a situation. Support persons can draw a social situation to facilitate understanding or assist the person on the spectrum in doing his own illustrations. It is not necessary to be a skillful artist to draw cartoons!

Tom, a young man with HF-ASD, was confused by conversations that girls were having with him. One in particular caused a meltdown. After Tom had regained self-control, his teacher asked him to relate the conversation that had distressed him while she cartooned what he said. Figure 4.5 shows Tom's conversation with a classmate, Mary, who had told him that he had a "cute butt." Tom, whose special interest was legal issues, thought he was being sexually harassed by Mary and called her a "sexist pig." Mary retorted by calling him a jerk. In kind, Tom repeated the comment. Tom's teacher helped him to understand, through the use of cartooning, that Mary was most likely trying to say that she liked Tom and that her feelings were hurt when she did not receive the expected response (an acknowledgment of her affection). The situation may have been further compounded when Mary was called a pig, particularly as she perceived herself as having a weight problem and might have interpreted this remark as being directed toward that issue. Following the session with his teacher, Tom was able to understand Mary's hidden message and that he had probably hurt her feelings. He then made plans to apologize to Mary for having misunderstood her. Adapted from Rogers & Myles (2001).

Tom at this point said to the author, "I don't think she's fat but I should not call her a pig. I need to tell her I'm sorry."

Figure 4.6. Cartoon.

From "Using Social Stories and Comic Strip Conversations to Interpret Social Situations for an Adolescent With Asperger Syndrome," by M. F. Rogers & B. S. Myles, 2001, *Intervention in School and Clinic, 36.* Used with permission.

Social Autopsies

Developed by LaVoie (cited in Bieber, 1994) to help individuals understand social mistakes and social successes, a social autopsy is used to dissect social incidents so that individuals learn from experiences. Social autopsies are particularly well suited to interpreting social and behavioral situations. After an event, the individual with HF-ASD and the support person analyze the components of a social situation, identifying correct and incorrect actions or words. If an error was made, together they develop a plan to ensure that it does not reoccur.

Because of the visual strengths of most persons on the spectrum, social autopsies may be enhanced by adding written words, phrases or pictorial representations to events. Lavoie overviewed the attributes and nonattributes of social autopsies, reiterating that it is a supportive, interpretive technique (see Table 4.4).

Table 4.4

Attributes and Nonattributes of Social Autopsies

A social autopsy is ...	A social autopsy is not ...
Supportive, structure, constructive	Punishment
Solution-oriented	Negative
An opportunity for the individual with HF-ASD to participate	Controlled by a support person
A process for interpretation	A "one-time" cure
Conducted after a social error or social success	
Led by an adult significant to the individual on the spectrum	
Generally held in a 1-on-1 session	

COACHING

Coaching, the third element in this multifaceted approach to intervention, recognizes that while some individuals on the spectrum know how to use a specific skill, they may not use it when appropriate. This may occur for a variety of reasons, including (a) difficulty generalizing the strategy to different settings, situations, and people; (b) experiencing a high level of stress that may cause the individual to temporarily "forget" the skills or not being able to recall the skills in the moment; and (c) forgetting how to begin the first step in the strategy. Coaching provides a "jump start" – a gentle nudge, a keyword, or a script that can prompt use of the strategy.

Coaching may take many forms. For example, a support person may:

- Point out someone at a social event who is alone and might want to interact socially. *"Marcus is standing over there by himself. I think that he might want someone to play with. Why don't you go over and talk to him."*

Note that the coach did not simply suggest *what* to do, but also provided a *why*.

- Provide the adult with HF-ASD a sentence or topic to use in a social exchange. *"Ask Libby if she has seen* [the latest superhero movie]. *If she has, you can say, 'What did you like about the movie?' If she says that she hasn't seen the movie, say, 'What movies have you seen lately?'"*

Some individuals with HF-ASD become highly anxious when they attempt to enter into a conversation or other social interaction and, in some cases, this anxiety is enough to trigger the meltdown cycle. Coaching provides a verbatim sentence or phrase that the person can use to get the conversation or social interaction started. Coaching may also include nonverbal cues. These simple cues may provide the support and encouragement the person needs in order to participate in the interaction rather than entering the rumbling stage.

For example, a coach and a person with HF-ASD might have a prearranged, discrete signal that cues the person to change topics, ask a question of a communicative partner, or move away from or toward someone, etc. Subtle signals include touching an earlobe or clearing the throat.

When selecting a signal, the support person must first ensure that the signal is readily noticeable to the individual but not to others in the environment. A second consideration is ensuring that the signal is not distracting. If the individual looks intently for the signal, he may not be able to engage in a conversation with a peer. In this case, the signal becomes more important than the social interaction and, therefore, is counterproductive.

OBSTACLE REMOVAL

Finally, obstacle removal, the fourth component of effective programming, involves modifying tasks and the environment. Ideally, the individual will learn over the years to remove obstacles in her environment (or request that they be removed) when possible, or to compensate for the presence of the obstacle so that she can continue to participate successfully. Obstacle removal includes the use of visual, peer, and environmental supports.

Visual Supports

As mentioned, most individuals with HF-ASD benefit from information that is presented visually rather than auditorily because it is more concrete and allows for greater processing time. In the following, we will look at visual schedules, graphic organizers, timelines, and maps as visual supports serving different purposes.

Visual schedules. Visual schedules take an abstract concept such as time and present it in a more concrete and manageable form, such as Penny's schedule in Figure 4.7.

Penny's Schedule	
Date: <u>Monday, December 8</u> ⬥Means there is a change and that's okay.	
8:00-8:15	Morning routine: ☐ Put away backpack ☐ Turn in homework ☐ Make lunch selection ☐ Take out journal ☐ Check helper chart
8:15-8:30	Write in journal
8:30-9:15	Math
9:15-10:00	Specials (circle one): Music Art P.E.
10:00-10:15	Restroom break
10:15-10:30	Snack and read book
10:30-11:00	Reading/Language Arts
11:00-11:30	Spelling
11:30-12:00	Lunch
12:00-12:30	Recess
12:30-1:00	Speech ⬥Library today because Ms. Jones is out sick
1:00-1:45	Science
1:45-2:15	Social Studies
2:15-2:30	Story time
2:30-2:45	Pack to go home
Thought for the day: Ms. Jones is out today, but that is okay. I will go to the library instead and see Ms. Jones on my speech day when she feels well.	

Figure 4.7. Student visual schedule.

From Aspy, R., & Grossman, B. G. (2011). *The Ziggurat model: A framework for designing comprehensive interventions for individuals with high-functioning autism and Asperger Syndrome* (2nd ed.) (p. 229). Shawnee Mission, KS: AAPC Publishing. Reprinted with permission.

As such, visual schedules can yield multiple benefits for those with HF-ASD, who often exhibit visual strengths. For example, visual schedules allow somebody to anticipate upcoming events and activities, develop an understanding of time, and facilitate the ability to predict change. Further, they can be utilized to stimulate communicative exchanges through a discussion of past, present, and future events; increase on-task behavior; facilitate transition between activities; and teach new skills.

Participation by the individual with HF-ASAD in preparing the schedule is often helpful. For example, a student can assist in assembling his schedule, copying it, or adding his own personal touch in some other manner. This interactive time can also be used to review the daily routine, discuss changes, and review expectations.

Figures 4.8 shows a schedule for an employee working at an Italian restaurant. If the individual is concerned about looking or acting differently from others, make sure that the schedule fits easily into the environment without attracting too much attention. For example, credit card-sized or bookmark-formatted visual schedules provide structure but can be used discreetly. Almost all well-functioning adults use a visual schedule or checklist to organize their day. In the real world, therefore, the presence of a visual schedule does not set a person apart, it helps him to fit in. On the other hand, the meltdown that may result from not knowing what to expect will quickly make an individual the center of unwanted attention.

Daily Schedule
Greet co-workers
Clock in
Wash hands
Put on apron
Make bread knots
Make pizza boxes
Fill napkins
Wrap utensils

Figure 4.8. Visual schedule for employee working in an Italian restaurant.

From Aspy, R., & Grossman, B. G. (personal communication, 2014). Used with permission.

Graphic organizers. Graphic organizers, such as semantic maps, Venn diagrams, outlines, and compare/contrast charts, provide visual, holistic representations of facts and concepts and their relationships within an organized framework. That is, these strategies arrange key terms to show their relationship to each other, presenting abstract or implicit information in a concrete manner. They are particularly useful with content-area material such as social studies, science, and so on, or tasks related to areas such as cooking, interviewing, and dating.

Graphic organizers often enhance the learning of those with HF-ASD because:

- They are visual – a frequent area of strength.

- They are static; they remain consistent and constant.

- They allow for processing time; the individual can reflect on the material at his own pace.

- They are concrete and are more easily understood than a verbal-only presentation.

Figure 4.9 provides an example of a graphic organizer that was created to help a young adult with HF-ASD understand the hidden meaning of what their boss said.

Friendly Things My Boss Says	Purely Friendly Comment	Comment With Hidden Meaning	Hidden Meaning
When you have time, please ...		X	You have no choice but to do whatever you are asked.
Good morning.	X		
It would be great if you could ...		X	This is usually a directive, meaning you will do whatever it is.

Figure 4.9. Graphic organizer: Hidden meaning of boss' statements.

From Myles, B. S., Endow, J., & Mayfield, M. (2013). *The hidden curriculum of getting and keeping a job: Navigating the social landscape of employment. A guide for individuals with autism spectrum disorders and other social-cognitive challenges* (p. 93). Shawnee Mission, KS: AAPC Publishing. Used with permission.

The graphic in Figure 4.10 was developed to help an adult male with HF-ASD understand that women sometimes focus more on feelings than facts than men do and that some men tend to focus more on facts.

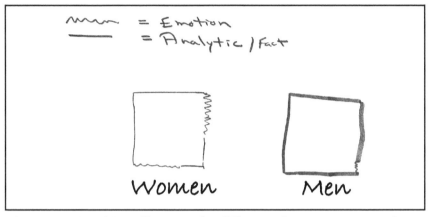

Figure 4.10. Graphic to illustrate the difference between men and women with regard to emotions vs. facts.

Timelines. Timelines – something most of us are faced with on a daily basis almost unconsciously – are another important form of visual support. Timelines break down assignments into their component parts and set deadlines for their completion. Because those with HF-ASD often have difficulty with the concept of time, many think they can read a novel and complete a 10-page project the night before it is due. Others simply cannot get started when given a complex task; they do not know, without assistance, how to break it down into smaller pieces. As a result, they spend the entire time worrying about getting the task done without having a strategy to begin and/or complete the task.

Maps. Maps are extremely important for persons with HF-ASD, particularly at the middle school and high school levels, when they cannot visualize where their locker is in reference to classes.

Josefa, a middle school student with HF-ASD, was on the verge of having to serve detention time for consistently being late to her classes. Following Josefa throughout her school day to determine the reason for her tardiness revealed that, very simply, Josefa was late to class because she went to her locker during each 10-minute passing time. For example, her second- and third-period classes were in the west wing of the building, but her locker was in the east wing. Instead of going to her locker after first period and gathering her books for the subsequent two periods, Josefa would race from the west wing to the east wing, and then back to the west wing after each class.

When given a map of the school showing her the most efficient ways to get from class to class and what books she should take with her each time she went to her locker, Josefa was able to change her pattern. Up until then, she had no idea that there was more than one way to get to any class, and she did not realize that it made more sense for her not to visit her locker between every class.

Peer Supports

Helping individuals with HF-ASD develop friendships and participate in support networks is integral to their success and often to their overall happiness. Because the desire for social interactions is typically high, involving the individual with peers is usually a strong motivator. In addition, it provides an excellent venue to practice social skills.

At times, it is necessary to help neurotypicals in the environment to understand some of the underlying needs of the individual with

HF-ASD, such as extra time to answer a question or saying their name first to get the attention of the individual with HF-ASD, and to equip them with some support strategies. Peer support can be designed to be a "two-way street." The individual with HF-ASD contributes strengths and skills while his partners contribute their strengths and skills. When peer supports are provided so that the individual with HF-ASD can interact successfully, positive relationships with peers become more likely.

Environmental Supports

Environmental supports can also enhance regulation. For example, to compensate for slow processing time, a student may complete only the even-numbered items on a math worksheet. Because of motor difficulties, some students may be permitted to take a test verbally or to type a book report on a tablet instead of writing it by hand. The adult who experiences problems with unaided recall may have a written or pictorial list of work tasks. The college student with HF-ASD who has difficulty remembering to do homework may use a calendar alert program on his phone.

Support staff should continually ask, "What can be done to make the environment more understandable for the individual? How can I help him be more successful?" The ultimate goal is to help individuals with HF-ASD to understand their exceptionality, complete with its strengths and challenges. From this understanding will come an awareness of the modifications the individual needs in order to be successful. Based on such understanding, the person on the spectrum can be taught to be active in putting into place modifications that will help her show her skills in a positive way.

SUMMARY

Helping individuals with HF-ASD to increase and enhance self-awareness, self-calming, and self-management requires a multifaceted approach. This includes instruction related to social, behavior, and academic skills; help in interpreting the environment; coaching to help use existing skills; and removing obstacles to ensure that individual needs are met. By using strategies in this chapter, individuals with HF-ASD will be better able to communicate their wants and needs and understand the often-challenging world. This understanding is likely to result in fewer meltdowns.

REFERENCES

Acar, C., & Diken, I. H. (2012). Reviewing instructional studies conducted using video modeling to children with autism. *Educational Sciences: Theory and Practice, 12*(4), 2731-2735.

Adams, J. I. (1997). *Autism-P.D.D.: More creative ideas from age eight to early adulthood.* Toronto, ONT, Canada: Adams Publications.

Albert, L. (1989). *A teacher's guide to cooperative discipline: How to manage your classroom and promote self-esteem.* Circle Pines, MN: American Guidance Service.

American Psychiatric Association. (2013). *Diagnostic and statistical manual of mental disorders* (5th ed.). Washington, DC: Author.

Arwood, E. L., & Kaulitz, C. (2007). *Learning with a visual brain in an auditory world: Visual language strategies for individuals with autism spectrum disorders.* Shawnee Mission, KS: AAPC Publishing.

Ashwin, C., Chapman, E., Howells, J., Rhydderch, D., Walker, I., & Baron-Cohen, S. (2014). Enhanced olfactory sensitivity in autism spectrum conditions. *Molecular Autism, 5*(1), 53.

Aspy, R., & Grossman, B. G. (2007, 2015). *Underlying characteristics checklist (five forms): Early intervention (EI); high-functioning (HF); classic (CL); self-report-adolescent (SR-Adol); self-report-adult (SR-Adult).* Shawnee Mission, KS: AAPC Publishing.

Aspy, R., & Grossman, B. G. (2011). *The Ziggurat model: A framework for designing comprehensive interventions for individuals with high-functioning autism and Asperger Syndrome* (2nd ed.). Shawnee Mission, KS: AAPC Publishing.

Aspy, R., Grossman, B. G., Myles, B. S., & Henry, S. A. (2016). *FBA to Z: Functional behavior assessment and intervention plans for individuals with ASD.* Shawnee Mission, KS: AAPC Publishing.

Baker, J. E. (2003). *Social skills training for children and adolescents with Asperger Syndrome and social communication problems.* Shawnee Mission, KS: AAPC Publishing.

Barnes, B., & Barnes, E. (2000). *A little book of manners for boys*. Eugene, OR: Harvest House Publishers.

Barnes, E. (1998). *A little book of manners: Courtesy & kindness for young ladies*. Eugene, OR: Harvest House Publishers.

Barnhill, G. P., Hagiwara, T., Myles, B. S., Simpson, R. L., Brick, M. L., & Griswold, D. E. (2000). Parent, teacher, and self-report of problem and adaptive behaviors in children and adolescents with Asperger syndrome. *Assessment for Effective Intervention, 25*(2), 147-167.

Baron-Cohen, S. (2007). *Mind reading: The interactive guide to emotions* [Version 1.3]. London, England: Jessica Kingsley.

Beck, M. (1985). Understanding and managing the acting out child. *The Pointer, 29*(2), 27-29.

Bellini, S. (2016). *Building social relationships 2*. Shawnee Mission, KS: AAPC Publishing.

Bennetto, L., Kuschner, E. S., & Hyman, S. L. (2007). Olfaction and taste processing in autism. *Biological Psychiatry, 62*(9), 1015-1021.

Benton, M., Hollis, C., Mahler, K., & Womer, A. (2011). *Destination friendship: Developing social skills for individuals with autism spectrum disorders or other social challenges*. Shawnee Mission, KS: AAPC Publishing.

Bieber, J. (Producer). (1994). *Learning disabilities and social skills with Richard LaVoie: Last one picked ... first one picked on*. Washington, DC: Public Broadcasting Service.

Billstedt, E., Gillberg, C., & Gillberg, C. (2005). Autism after adolescence: Population-based 13- to 22-year follow-up study of 120 individuals with autism diagnosed in childhood. *Journal of Autism and Developmental Disorders, 35*(3), 351-360.

Bridges, J., & Curtis, B. (2012). *As a gentleman would say: Revised and expanded*. Nashville, TN: Rutledge Hill Press.

Buron, K. D., Brown, J. T., Curtis, M., & King, L. (2012). *Social behavior and self-management: 5-point scales for adolescents and adults.* Shawnee Mission, KS: AAPC Publishing.

Buron, K. D., & Curtis, M. (2012). *The Incredible 5-Point Scale: The significantly improved and expanded second edition.* Shawnee Mission, KS: AAPC Publishing.

Campbell, A., & Tincani, M. (2011). The Power Card strategy: Strength-based intervention to increase direction following of children with autism spectrum disorder. *Journal of Positive Behavior Interventions, 13*(4), 240-249.

Cardon, T. A. (2004). *Let's talk emotions: Helping children with social cognitive deficits, including AS, HFA, and NVLD, learn to understand and express empathy and emotions.* Shawnee Mission, KS: AAPC Publishing.

Case-Smith, J., Weaver, L. L., & Fristad, M. A. (2015). A systematic review of sensory processing interventions for children with autism spectrum disorders. *Autism, 19*(2), 133-148.

Coucouvanis, J. (2005). *Super skills: A social skills group program for children with Asperger Syndrome, high-functioning autism and related challenges.* Shawnee Mission, KS: AAPC Publishing.

Davis, K. M., Boon, R. T., Cihak, D. F., & Fore III, C. (2010). Power Cards to improve conversation skills in adolescents with Asperger Syndrome. *Focus on Autism and Developmental Disorders, 25,* 12-22.

Diamond, S. (2011). *Social rules for kids: The top 100 social rules kids need to succeed.* Shawnee Mission, KS: AAPC Publishing.

Donvan, J., & Zucker, K. (2016). *In a different key: The story of autism.* New York, NY: Crown.

Espeland, P. (2003). *Life lists for teens.* Minneapolis, MN: Free Spirit Publishing, Inc.

Fitzgerald, M., & O'Brien, B. (2007). *Genius genes: How Asperger talents changed the world.* Shawnee Mission, KS: AAPC Publishing.

Flanagan, M. (2016). *Strategies for successful mealtimes: A program for children with autism spectrum and related disorders who have eating difficulties.* Shawnee Mission, KS: AAPC Publishing.

Gagnon, E., & Myles, B. S. (2016). *The Power Card strategy 2: Using special interests to motivate children and youth with autism spectrum disorder.* Shawnee Mission, KS: AAPC Publishing.

Ganz, J. B., Kaylor, M., Bourgeois, B., & Hadden, K. (2008). The impact of social scripts and visual cues on verbal communication in three children with autism spectrum disorders. *Focus on Autism and Other Developmental Disabilities, 23,* 79-94.

Ghaziuddin, N., Dhossche, D., & Marcotte, K. (2012). Retrospective chart review of catatonia in child and adolescent psychiatric patients. *Acta Psychiatrica Scandinavica, 125*(1), 33-38.

Grandin, T. (1999, April). *Understanding people with autism: Developing a career makes life satisfying.* Paper presented at the MAAP Services, Incorporated, and Indiana Resource Center for Autism Conference, Indianapolis, IN.

Gray, C. (1994). *Comic strip conversations*™. Arlington, TX: Future Horizons.

Green, S. A., Hernandez, L., Tottenham, N., Krasileva, K., Bookheimer, S. Y., & Dapretto, M. (2015). Neurobiology of sensory overresponsivity in youth with autism spectrum disorders. *JAMA Psychiatry.* doi:10/1001/jamapsychiatry.2015.0737

Green, S. A., Rudie, J. D., Colich, N. L., Wood, J. J., Shirinyan, D., Hernandez, L., ... & Bookheimer, S. Y. (2013). Overreactive brain responses to sensory stimuli in youth with autism spectrum disorders. *Journal of the American Academy of Child & Adolescent Psychiatry, 52*(11), 1158-1172.

Kauchak, T. (2002). *I can do anything!: Smart cards for strong girls.* Middleton, WI: Pleasant Company Publications.

Kirchner, J. C., & Dziobek, I. (2014). Towards successful employment of adults with autism: A first analysis of special interests and factors deemed important for vocational performance. *Scandinavian Journal of Child and Adolescent Psychiatry and Psychology, 2*(2), 77-85.

Klipper, B., & Shapiro-Rieser, R. (2015). *The secret rules of social networking.* Shawnee Mission, KS: AAPC Publishing.

Kohls, G., Schulte-Rüther, M., Nehrkorn, B., Müller, K., Fink, G. R., Kamp-Becker, I., ... & Konrad, K. (2012). Reward system dysfunction in autism spectrum disorders. *Social Cognitive and Affective Neuroscience*, nss033.

Koshino, H., Kana, R. K., Keller, T. A., Cherkassky, V. L., Minshew, N. J., & Just, M. A. (2008). fMRI investigation of working memory for faces in autism: visual coding and underconnectivity with frontal areas. *Cerebral Cortex, 18*(2), 289-300.

Ledgin, N. (2002). *Asperger's and self-esteem: Insight and hope through famous role models.* Arlington, TX: Future Horizons.

Lequia, J., Machalicek, W., & Rispoli, M. J. (2012). Effects of activity schedules on challenging behavior exhibited in children with autism spectrum disorders: A systematic review. *Research in Autism Spectrum Disorders, 6*(1), 480-492.

Long, N. J., Morse, W. C., & Newman, R. G. (1976). *Conflict in the classroom: The educational children with problems* (3rd ed.). Belmont, CA: Wadsworth.

Madden, K. (2002). *Writing smarts: A girl's guide to writing great poetry, stories, school reports, and more!* Middleton, WI: Pleasant Company Publications.

Madison, L., & Masse, J. (2013). *The feelings book: The care & keeping of your emotions* (2nd ed). Middleton, WI: Pleasant Company Publications.

Mahler, K. (2015). *Interoception: The eighth sense: Practical solution for improving self-awareness and social understanding in individuals with autism spectrum and related disorders.* Shawnee Mission, KS: AAPC Publishing.

Marco, E. J., Hinkley, L. B., Hill, S. S., & Nagarajan, S. S. (2011). Sensory processing in autism: A review of neurophysiologic findings. *Pediatric Research, 69*, 48R-54R.

Marko, M. K., Crocetti, D., Hulst, T., Donchin, O., Shadmehr, R., & Mostofsky, S. H. (2015). Behavioural and neural basis of anomalous motor learning in children with autism. *Brain, 138*(3), 784-797.

McAfee, J. (2002). *Navigating the social world: A curriculum for individuals with Asperger's Syndrome, high functioning autism, and related disorders.* Arlington, TX: Future Horizons.

Moss, P., Howlin, P., Savage, S., Bolton, P., & Rutter, M. (2015). Self and informant reports of mental health difficulties among adults with autism findings from a long-term follow-up study. *Autism, 19*(7), 832-841.

Myles, B. S., Endow, J., & Mayfield, M. (2013). *The hidden curriculum of getting and keeping a job: Navigating the social landscape of employment. A guide for individuals with autism spectrum disorders and other social-cognitive challenges.* Shawnee Mission, KS: AAPC Publishing.

Myles, B. S., Hagiwara, T., Dunn, W., Rinner, L., Reese, M., Huggins, A., & Becker, J. (2004). Sensory issues in children with Asperger Syndrome and autism. *Education and Training in Developmental Disabilities, 3*(4), 283-290.

Myles, B. S., Mahler, K., & Robbins, L. A. (2014). *Sensory issues and high functioning autism spectrum and related disorders: Practical solutions for making sense of the world.* Shawnee Mission, KS: AAPC Publishing.

Myles, B. S., & Southwick, J. (2005). *Asperger syndrome and difficult moments – practical solutions for tantrums, rage, and meltdowns* (pp. 59-62). Shawnee Mission, KS: AAPC Publishing.

Myles, B. S., Trautman, M. L., & Schelvan, R. L. (2013). *The hidden curriculum: Practical solutions for understanding unstated rules in social situations* (2nd ed.). Shawnee Mission, KS: AAPC Publishing.

Myles, H., & Kolar, A. (2013). *The hidden curriculum and other everyday challenges for elementary children with high-functioning autism.* Shawnee Mission, KS: AAPC Publishing.

Northoff, G. (2000). Brain imaging in catatonia: Current findings and a pathophysiologic model. *CNS Spectrums, 5*(07), 34-46.

Packer, A. J. (2014). *How rude! The teenager's guide to good manners, proper behavior, and not grossing people out* (2nd ed.). Minneapolis, MN: Free Spirit Publishing.

Prizant, B. (2015). *Uniquely human: A different way of seeing autism.* New York, NY: Simon & Schuster.

Raymer, D. (2015). *A smart girl's guide: Staying home alone: A girl's guide to feeling safe and having fun.* Middleton, WI: Pleasant Company Publications.

Richey, J. A., Damiano, C. R., Sabatino, A., Rittenberg, A., Petty, C., Bizzell, J., ... & Dichter, G. S. (2015). Neural mechanisms of emotion regulation in autism spectrum disorder. *Journal of Autism and Developmental Disorders*, 1-15.

Rogers, M. F., & Myles, B. S. (2001). Using social stories and comic strip conversations to interpret social situations for an adolescent with Asperger Syndrome. *Intervention in School and Clinic, 36*(5), 310-313.

Schaefer, V. L., & Masse, J. (2012). *The care & keeping of you: The body book for younger girls* (2nd ed.). Middleton, WI: Pleasant Company Publications.

Schopler, E. (1994). Behavioral priorities for autism and related developmental disorders. In E. Schopler & G. B. Mesibov (Eds.), *Behavioral issues in autism* (pp. 55-75). New York, NY: Plenum Press.

Silberman, S. (2015a). *Neurotribes: The legacy of autism and the future of neurodiverstiy*. New York, NY: Avery.

Silberman, S. (2015b). Steve Silberman: Author of Neurotribes: The legacy of autism and the future of neurodiversity. Retrieved from http://stevesilberman.com/book/neurotribes/

Smith, V., & Jelen, M. (2010). Social scripts and visual cues for children with ASD: More evidence for increasing context appropriate conversation and suggested collateral effects. *Evidence-Based Communication Assessment and Intervention, 4*(1), 32-36.

Soulières, I., Dawson, M., Samson, F., Barbeau, E. B., Sahyoun, C. P., Strangman, G. E., ... & Mottron, L. (2009). Enhanced visual processing contributes to matrix reasoning in autism. *Human Brain Mapping, 30*(12), 4082-4107.

Tiger, C. (2003). *How to behave: A guide to modern manners for the socially challenged*. Philadelphia, PA: Quirk Books.

Tomchek, S. D., & Dunn, W. (2007). Sensory processing in children with and without autism: A comparative study using the Short Sensory Profile. *The American Journal of Occupational Therapy, 61,* 190-200.

Vermeulen, P. (2012). *Autism as context blindness*. Shawnee Mission, KS: AAPC Publishing.

Winner, M. G. (2002). *Thinking about you, thinking about me: Philosophy and strategies to further develop perspective taking and communicative abilities for persons with social cognitive deficits*. San Jose, CA: Author.

Winter-Messiers, M. (2007). From tarantulas to toilet brushes: Understanding the special interest areas of children and youth with Asperger's syndrome. *Remedial and Special Education, 28,* 140-152.

Wolfberg, P. J. (2003). *Peer play and the autism spectrum: The art of guiding children's socialization and imagination*. Shawnee Mission, KS: AAPC Publishing.

APPENDIX

Student Crisis Plan Sheet

Student Name_____   Student Age/Grade_____

Teacher Name_____   Date of Plan _____

ENVIRONMENTAL/PERSONNEL CONSIDERATIONS

1. Describe how you can obtain assistance when it is needed_____
   _____
   _____

2. At which stage should outside assistance be sought?

   _____ rumbling   _____ rage   _____ recovery

3. Which school personnel are available to provide assistance?

   _____ principal   _____ school psychologist   _____ paraprofessional
   _____ social worker   _____ counselor
   _____ other (please specify)_____
   _____ other (please specify)_____

4. Where should child(ren) exit to? (specify room or school)_____

5. At what stage should the plan be used by others in the classroom?

   _____ rumbling   _____ rage   _____ recovery

6. Are there any extenuating circumstances that others should know about this student (i.e., medications, related medical conditions, home situation)?

7. Who should be notified of the incident?_____

8. How should the incident be documented?_____

From Myles, B. S., & Southwick, J. (2005). *Asperger syndrome and difficult moments – practical solutions for tantrums, rage, and meltdowns* (pp. 59-62). Shawnee Mission, KS: AAPC Publishing. Used with permission.

RUMBLING STAGE

1. What environmental factors/activities or antecedents lead to "rumbling" behaviors?

_____ unplanned change _____ difficult assignment _____ crowds
_____ teacher criticism _____ transitions _____ conflict with classmate
_____ other (please describe)_____

2. What behaviors does the student exhibit during the rumbling stage?

_____ bites nails _____ tenses muscles _____ stares
_____ taunts others _____ refuses to work _____ fidgets
_____ other (please describe)_____
_____ other (please describe)_____

3. Does the student mention any of the following complaints or illness?

_____ stomachache _____ headache _____ not applicable
_____ other (please describe)_____

4. Should the student be sent to the nurse if there is a complaint of illness?

_____ yes _____ no

5. How long does the rumbling stage last before it progresses to the next stage?

_____

6. What interventions should be used at this stage?

_____ antiseptic bouncing _____ proximity control _____ touch control
_____ "just walk and don't talk" _____ home base _____ redirecting
_____ other (please specify)_____
_____

_____ other (please specify)_____
_____

From Myles, B. S., & Southwick, J. (2005). *Asperger syndrome and difficult moments – practical solutions for tantrums, rage, and meltdowns* (pp. 59-62). Shawnee Mission, KS: AAPC Publishing. Used with permission.

RAGE STAGE

1. What behaviors does the student exhibit during the rage stage?

_____ student verbally lashes   _____ student verbally lashes
out at teacher   out at other students
_____ student threatens to hit teacher   _____ student threatens to hit students
_____ student destroys materials   _____ student attempts to leave
classroom
_____ student withdraws from teacher   _____ student hurts self
_____ other (please specify)_____
_____ other (please specify)_____

2. What teacher interventions should be used during this stage?

_____ physically move child to safe room   _____ prompt child to move to safe room
_____ remove others from the classroom   _____ redirect student
_____ other (please specify)_____
_____ other (please specify)_____

3. What is the role of others in the child's environment during the rage stage?
_____
_____

RECOVERY STAGE

1. What behaviors does the student exhibit during the recovery stage without intervention?

_____ sullenness   _____ withdrawal into fantasy   _____ denial
_____ "typical" student behavior
_____ other (please describe) _____
_____ other (please describe) _____

2. What supportive techniques should be used during this stage?
_____
_____

3. What interventions should be used at a later time to assist the student in gaining more self-control?_____

From Myles, B. S., & Southwick, J. (2005). *Asperger syndrome and difficult moments – practical solutions for tantrums, rage, and meltdowns* (pp. 59-62). Shawnee Mission, KS: AAPC Publishing. Used with permission.

Crisis Report Form

Student Name_____

Teacher Name_____

Setting_____ Date _____

Antecedent Events_____

Rumbling Stage

Student Behavior_____

_____

Teacher Interventions_____

_____

Rage Stage

Student Behavior_____

_____

Teacher Interventions_____

_____

Recovery Stage

Student Behavior_____

_____

Teacher Interventions_____

_____

Other Considerations

_____

_____

From Myles, B. S., & Southwick, J. (2005). *Asperger syndrome and difficult moments – practical solutions for tantrums, rage, and meltdowns* (pp. 59-62). Shawnee Mission, KS: AAPC Publishing. Used with permission.

Related Books From AAPC ...

Your First Source for Practical Solutions for Autism Spectrum and Related Disorders

Super Skills: A Social Skills Group Program for Children With Asperger Syndrome, High-Functioning Autism and Related Challenges by Coucouvanis (2005).

Social Skills Training for Children and Adolescents With Asperger Syndrome and Other Social Communication Problems by Baker (2003).

Building Social Relationships 2 by Bellini (2016).

Destination Friendship by Benton, Hollis, Mahler, and Womer (2011).

 *Let's Talk Emotions: Helping Children With Social Cognitive Deficits, Including AS, HFA, and NVLD, Learn to Understand and Express Empathy and Emotions* by Cardon (2004).

 *Social Rules for Kids: The Top 100 Social Rules Kids Need to Succeed* by Diamond (2011).

 *Peer Play and the Autism Spectrum: The Art of Guiding Children's Socialization and Imagination* by Wolfberg (2003).

 *The Secret Rules of Social Networking* by Klipper & Shapiro-Rieser (2015).

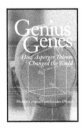 *Genius Genes: How Asperger Challenges Changed the World* by Fitzgerald and O'Brien (2007).

www.aapcpublishing.net

11209 Strang Line Rd.
Lenexa, Kansas 66215
www.aapcpublishing.net

CPSIA information can be obtained
at www.ICGtesting.com
Printed in the USA
LVHW022327070519
617050LV00015B/243/P